THE EVERYTHING®
GUIDE TO WRITING
Graphic Novels

Dear Reader,

You have begun a challenging journey of creation, but a long road does not necessarily mean you will not reach your destination. We admire your courage and dedication, your desire to create something lasting and memorable from your unique vision of the world.

Just as the journey of a thousand miles begins with a single step, so does the creation of a graphic novel begin with a commitment to reaching a specific goal, panel by panel, page by page. We have been on that road ourselves, but this book can be your guide and, hopefully, keep you from getting lost along the way.

Safe journey!

Mark Ellis

Melissa Martin Ellis

Welcome to the EVERYTHING® Series!

These handy, accessible books give you all you need to tackle a difficult project, gain a new hobby, comprehend a fascinating topic, prepare for an exam, or even brush up on something you learned back in school but have since forgotten.

You can choose to read an *Everything*® book from cover to cover or just pick out the information you want from our four useful boxes: e-questions, e-facts, e-alerts, e-ssentials. We give you everything you need to know on the subject, but throw in a lot of fun stuff along the way, too.

We now have more than 400 *Everything*® books in print, spanning such wide-ranging categories as weddings, pregnancy, cooking, music instruction, foreign language, crafts, pets, New Age, and so much more. When you're done reading them all, you can finally say you know *Everything*®!

E-QUESTION

Answers to common questions

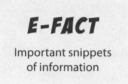

E-FACT

Important snippets of information

E-ALERT

Urgent warnings

E-SSENTIAL

Quick handy tips

DIRECTOR OF INNOVATION Paula Munier

EDITORIAL DIRECTOR Laura M. Daly

EXECUTIVE EDITOR, SERIES BOOKS Brielle K. Matson

ASSOCIATE COPY CHIEF Sheila Zwiebel

ACQUISITIONS EDITOR Lisa Laing

DEVELOPMENT EDITOR Katie McDonough

PRODUCTION EDITOR Casey Ebert

Visit the entire Everything® series at **www.everything.com**

THE
EVERYTHING®
GUIDE TO
WRITING
GRAPHIC NOVELS

FROM SUPERHEROES TO MANGA—ALL YOU NEED
TO CREATE AND SELL YOUR GRAPHIC WORKS

MARK ELLIS AND MELISSA MARTIN ELLIS

Adamsmedia
AVON, MASSACHUSETTS

*This book is dedicated to all those who have the spark
of creativity within them, the shapers and creators of
imaginary worlds. Your dreams can become reality.*

Copyright © 2008 by F+W Publications, Inc. All rights reserved.
This book, or parts thereof, may not be reproduced
in any form without permission from the publisher; exceptions
are made for brief excerpts used in published reviews.

An Everything® Series Book.
Everything® and everything.com® are registered trademarks of F+W Publications, Inc.

Published by Adams Media, an F+W Publications Company
57 Littlefield Street, Avon, MA 02322 U.S.A.
www.adamsmedia.com

ISBN 10: 1-58969-451-0
ISBN: 978-1-59869-451-2

Printed in the United States of America.

J I H G F E D C B A

Library of Congress Cataloging-in-Publication Data
is available from the publisher.

*This book is available at quantity discounts for bulk purchases.
For information, please call 1-800-289-0963.*

CONTENTS

TOP TEN BOOKS EVERY GRAPHIC NOVELIST SHOULD READ

1. *Graphic Storytelling and Visual Narrative*

   by Will Eisner

2. *Understanding Comics: The Invisible Art*

   by Scott McLeod

3. *How to Draw Comics the Marvel Way*

   by Stan Lee and John Buscema

4. *The DC Comics Guide to Writing Comics*

   by Denny O'Neil

5. *Milton Caniff: Conversations*

   by Milton Caniff and R. C. Harvey

6. *The Dark Knight Returns*

   by Frank Miller and Lynn Varley

7. *Watchmen*

   by Alan Moore and Dave Gibbons

8. *Kingdom Come*

   by Kurt Busiek and Alex Ross

9. *V for Vendetta*

   by Alan Moore and David Lloyd

10. *Blueberry: Chihuahua Pearl*

    by Jean-Michel Charlier and Moebius

INTRODUCTION

COMICS HISTORIAN, artist, and visionary Jim Steranko described the genesis of modern comic books as a "dream that instantly developed into a full-scale industry." More than just a cultural phenomenon, comic books became, along with jazz, a uniquely American art form. Like jazz, comics suffered through a long period of time when they were considered disreputable.

Although the comics form entered into popular culture far more swiftly than jazz, it was never accorded any degree of respect and was usually dismissed as an example of completely disposable art. People who found value in the comics medium, either as fans or creators, were viewed as little better than subliterates.

But, as the old song says, time was on our side. In the form of the graphic novel, the comics medium is now a legitimate expression of both art and literature. The creative urge can find its full outlet through the marriage of narrative and sequential art, melding drawing and story elements into something unique—a tale told through pictures and dialogue, separated into single images confined by panels.

Although comic books have been traditionally produced by a team (writer, pencil artist, inker, colorist, and letterer), very often graphic novels harken back to the older production method of newspaper strips. These features were created by writer-artists like Milton Caniff, Will Eisner, and Hal Foster. They were artists, but they were also blessed with the talent to spin gripping yarns. These were young men who started out with a dream and many pictures later found themselves to be the authors of enduring pieces of Americana, parents of cultural icons that have outlived their creators. The authors of today's graphic novels may very well find that their own dreams will achieve a similar sort of immortality.

The Everything® Guide to Writing Graphic Novels outlines the process of comics' creation, from story to panel layout to finished, printed production. Graphic novels have entered the mainstream and are a hot category for both established professionals and aspiring creators. From superheroes to werewolves, Hollywood is increasingly looking to adapt graphic novels into films. *V for Vendetta, Road to Perdition, A History of Violence, The Watchmen*—

these are just a few graphic novels that have enjoyed immense popularity and translation into big-budget films.

This book breaks down the process into easy-to-follow steps, from the creation of characters to gripping storylines to the ins and outs of publication and production. You'll find examples of comics' artwork by famous, even legendary, artists to use as guides and inspirations. At the same time, you'll get a little of the same kind of emotional nourishment provided by comics themselves—a sense of fun and adventure.

Acknowledgments

To the immortals: Jim Mooney, Milton Caniff, Hal Foster, Jack Kirby, Don Heck, and Will Eisner—geniuses and trailblazers of the industry. Thanks for showing us how it can and should be done.

CHAPTER 1

HOW GRAPHIC NOVELS CAME TO BE

As the old adage goes, a picture is worth a thousand words. Combine those thousand words with an equal number of pictures, and you have that uniquely American art form known as the graphic novel. The comics format, telling a story through pictures, is nothing new. It is as old as the creative urge. To tell a story using sequential art is both simple and complex, and that choice depends entirely upon the storyteller. This chapter looks back at the evolution of the medium from a compilation of newspaper strips to today's sophisticated graphic novels.

From Funny Books to Graphic Novels

Funny book is a term now as quaint as *groovy* or *fab*. The word derives from the mid-1930s when comic magazines were only reprints of newspaper funny pages. At that time, comic books jammed Flash Gordon shoulder to shoulder with Popeye. The reading public was happy

© 1935 DC Comics, art by Lynne Anderson.

▲ *New Fun* #1 was the first American comic book with all original material.

with this arrangement, because, after all, it was only a book that contained the "funnies," and there was no stigma attached to reading the funny papers.

It might have gone on that way, except the reprint and licensing fees to the comic strip syndication companies became exorbitant. Major Malcolm Wheeler-Nicholson, founder of DC Comics, decided the best way to cut costs was to publish magazines containing new, original material.

In 1935, the first issue of *New Fun* appeared. At the time, Major Wheeler-Nicholson had no idea that this single publication defined the modern comic book and created a new medium of entertainment and artistic expression. In a short time, the term *funny book* gave way to *comic book*.

Comic Book Superheroes

DC further established its influence on popular culture in 1938 when the company published the first issue of *Action Comics,* which featured the introduction of Superman. The creation of two teenagers from Ohio, Joe Shuster and Jerry Siegel, Superman kicked off an entirely new genre that became forever linked with comic books—the superhero.

The early Superman stories were crude but exuberant statements on the plight of the common man facing the uncertain world of the Depression. The days were bleak and liberal sentiments ran high.

Art by Jim Mooney.

LIGHTNING RECEIVED THE GIFT OF SPEED, STRENGTH AND POWER OF LIGHTNING FROM THE OLD MAN OF THE PYRAMIDS, IN ANCIENT EGYPT, IN ORDER THAT HE MIGHT WAGE A MIGHTY CRUSADE AGAINST CRIME

◀ "Flash" Lightning was one of the many superheroes who appeared during the comic book boom of the 1940s.

Superman symbolized the frustration of the downtrodden and the poverty stricken. The character was such a powerful reflection of the times that adults as well as children followed his adventures.

E-SSENTIAL

IN 1933, OHIO NATIVES JERRY SIEGEL AND JOE SHUSTER CREATED WHAT IS INARGUABLY THE INDUSTRY'S MOST WELL-KNOWN CHARACTER, SUPERMAN, WHILE THEY WERE STILL IN THEIR TEENS. THE PAIR WERE UNABLE TO INTEREST A PUBLISHER IN THE CHARACTER, HOWEVER, UNTIL 1938 WHEN DC NEEDED MATERIAL TO FILL OUT THE FIRST ISSUE OF ACTION COMICS.

The Man of Steel sparked the first superhero mania, popularly known as the golden age of comics. During the comic book boom of the 1940s, characters in masks and capes appeared and disappeared with a dizzying frequency. DC cornered the market with their iconic characters such as Batman and Wonder Woman.

The number of monthly comic books produced by various publishers soared into the millions. Many of them featured cheap imitations of Superman, Batman, and Wonder Woman, and only a handful survived beyond the golden age.

New Genres Appear

By the end of World War II, the market was so saturated with superfolk publishers turned to other genres, putting out everything from educational comics to romance stories. The creators were by and large young cartoonists who aspired to become newspaper strip artists, like the immensely popular Milton Caniff, Alex Raymond, and Hal Foster.

Terry and the Pirates by Milton Caniff, who was considered the "Rembrandt of the Comic Strip."

E-FACT

IN THE EARLY 1950S, AT THE HEIGHT OF THE COMICS BOOM, WHEN PAPER WAS CHEAP AND PRINTING COSTS WERE A FRACTION OF WHAT THEY ARE TODAY, INDUSTRY-WIDE SALES OF COMIC BOOKS WERE ESTIMATED AT 70 MILLION TO 150 MILLION COPIES PER MONTH, A REMARKABLE FIGURE COMPARED TO TODAY'S SALES FIGURES OF AROUND 6 TO 7 MILLION PER MONTH.

© 2006 Chicago Tribune Syndicate.

Dark Times

Unfortunately, during the late 1940s the reputation of comics sank. The low-priced, cheaply printed periodicals with garish covers were associated with subpar literacy levels among children, and by the early 1950s they were even accused of contributing to juvenile delinquency. This stigma remained with comics until the mid-to-late 1960s, when the fledgling Marvel Comics Group became popular with college students.

E-FACT

SEDUCTION OF THE INNOCENT, A BOOK BY CHILD PSYCHIATRIST FREDRIC WERTHAM PUBLISHED IN 1954, BLAMED JUVENILE DELINQUENCY ON CRIME COMIC BOOKS. WERTHAM'S ACCUSATIONS SPARKED A SENATE HEARING, AND THE PUBLIC OUTCRY RESULTED IN A SELF-CENSORING BODY CALLED THE COMICS CODE AUTHORITY. LAWS RESTRICTING THE SALE OF COMICS WERE INTRODUCED IN EIGHTEEN STATES.

Coming of Age

Another generation passed before the comics medium and the art of graphic storytelling was accepted as a legitimate form. By the 1990s, the term *comic book* had been replaced in favor of *graphic novel* when talking about a publication that contained a complete story arc and an expanded page format of at least ninety pages. Although the difference between the two was primarily a matter of packaging, the term *graphic novel* denoted a higher-end publication, usually with slicker production values.

⚠ The seal of the Comics Code Authority, which appeared on books approved by them.

Defining the Form

What separates graphic novels from other comics isn't strictly defined. Generally a graphic novel is considered to be a self-contained story that has a beginning, middle, and end, addressing more mature themes than traditional comic books.

Graphic novels usually have higher production values as opposed to mass-produced comics. Comic historians consider *He Done Her Wrong*, by cartoonist Milt Gross, to be the first American graphic novel. It was published in 1930, years before the debut of Superman.

E-FACT

IN 1968, GIL KANE AND ARCHIE GOODWIN SELF-PUBLISHED A FORTY-PAGE COMICS NOVEL ENTITLED *HIS NAME IS—SAVAGE!* A FEW YEARS LATER, KANE AND GOODWIN'S SCIENCE FICTION/SWORD AND SORCERY 119-PAGE GRAPHIC NOVEL, *BLACKMARK* (1971), WAS PUBLISHED AS A STANDARD-SIZE PAPERBACK NOVEL BY BANTAM, WHICH WAS A VERY UNUSUAL MOVE FOR THE TIME.

Unlike the magazine format of comic books, a graphic novel is typically bound like a standard prose novel, sometimes with both softcover and hardcover editions. They are sold in bookstores as well as specialty comic book shops. They also have a much longer shelf life and remain in print longer.

Building Momentum

Graphic novels have been available in some shape or form for a long time. Milton Caniff often referred to his *Terry and the Pirates* and *Steve Canyon* newspaper strips as open-ended "picaresque novels." Extended story arcs from both features were often compiled and packaged in single volumes.

The actual term *graphic novel* wasn't popularized until 1978 when the two words appeared on the cover of the paperback edition of Will Eisner's groundbreaking *A Contract with God and Other Tenement Stories*. Shortly after that, the term fell into common usage.

In many ways, the advent of the graphic novel is credited with saving the comics field, raising the medium's profile to a new, respectable level. Frank Miller's *Batman: The Dark Knight Returns* made the *New York Times* bestseller list and garnered a considerable amount of positive attention from the mainstream press.

E-SSENTIAL

MANGA, THE JAPANESE VERSION OF GRAPHIC NOVELS, HAS BEEN PUBLISHED SINCE THE 1950S. EUROPE BEGAN PUBLISHING ORIGINAL GRAPHIC NOVELS IN THE EARLY 1960S WITH BOOK-LENGTH STORIES. IN AMERICA A FEW COMIC BOOK CREATORS BEGAN EXPERIMENTING WITH THE FORM, HOPING TO STRETCH THE PARAMETERS.

In 1987, Alan Moore and Dave Gibbons's *Watchmen*, a revisionistic take on superheroes, was hailed as a revolutionary step forward in the maturity of the genre. In the late 1980s, both Marvel and DC began ambitious graphic novel programs.

Other publishers quickly followed suit with unconventional material such as Art Spiegelman's *Maus* and autobiographical works such as *American Splendor* by Harvey Pekar.

E-FACT

WATCHMEN IS THE ONLY GRAPHIC NOVEL TO APPEAR ON *TIME* MAGAZINE'S *2005* LIST OF THE ONE HUNDRED BEST ENGLISH-LANGUAGE NOVELS FROM 1923 TO THE PRESENT. IT HELPED TO POPULARIZE THE GRAPHIC NOVEL FORMAT AND WON A HUGO AWARD FOR ALAN MOORE AND DAVE GIBBONS.

Current Trends

Unlike the standard prose novel, graphic novels aren't bound by marketplace trends. However, since the medium is primarily visual, the quality and style of the artwork and the narrative is both the package and the product.

Movie Adaptations

The types of stories in graphic novels are limited only by the imaginations and artistic skills of their creators, which makes graphic novels one of the very few media with built-in cross-platform elements.

Hollywood producers are attracted to graphic novels for a variety of reasons, not the least of which is that a potential film is already storyboarded. A graphic novel is much easier to visualize as a movie than a book or even a script. Take a look at the number of movies adapted from graphic novels over the last few years:

- *A History of Violence* by John Wagner and Vince Locke
- *Ghost World* by Daniel Clowes

The Miskatonic Project © 2006 Mark Ellis.

🔺 This panel sequence by Don Heck from *The Whisperer in Darkness* typifies the cinematic visuals that make graphic novels attractive to moviemakers.

- *Road to Perdition* by Max Allan Collins and Richard Piers Rayner
- *Art School Confidential* by Daniel Clowes
- *From Hell* by Alan Moore and Eddie Campbell
- *The League of Extraordinary Gentlemen* by Alan Moore and Kevin O'Neill
- *The Rocketeer* by Dave Stevens
- *Sin City* by Frank Miller
- *V for Vendetta* by Alan Moore and David Lloyd
- *The Crow* by James O'Barr

In fact, a graphic novel conference was organized a few years ago in New York City that featured filmmaker and comics writer Kevin Smith as the celebrity guest. The conference brought together industry professionals to discuss the business and cultural facets of graphic novels, from Japanese manga to superhero comics.

Obviously, superheroes such as those published by Marvel and DC will always be a major presence in the graphic narrative format, particularly as more movies are based on their characters and the publications reach wider audiences. According to *Publishers Weekly*, retail graphic novel sales were around $245 million in 2005, an 18 percent increase from 2004.

▶ The scope of graphic novels are limited only by the imaginations of the creators.

Mainstream Media

Bookstores, publishers, and mainstream cultural venues are devoting more resources to graphic novels. They can be found in Borders, Barnes & Noble, and online as promotional collateral for television shows such as *Heroes*. But just as popular culture is diverse, so are the genres featured in graphic novels.

With graphic novels, the sky isn't the limit; the boundaries extend to all times and places and the stretches of the universe itself.

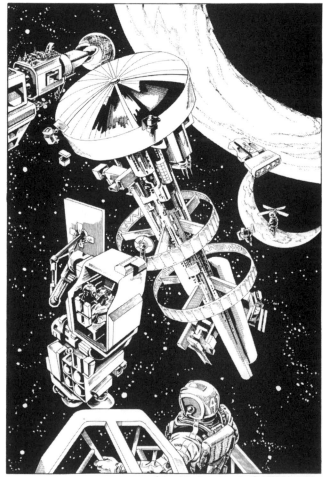

Artwork by Robert Lewis, © 2006 Mark Ellis.

CHAPTER 2

DO YOU HAVE WHAT IT TAKES?

Although a journey of a thousand miles may begin with a first step, preparation for the journey precedes it. Comfortable walking shoes have to be bought, maps consulted, routes planned, and research performed. Regardless of the kind of story you want to tell in your graphic novel, research is a necessity if for no other reason than to figure out what will grab and hold a potential audience. This chapter covers all the resources and skills you'll need on your journey as a graphic novelist, from financial requirements to time-management skills.

Death Hawk ©Mark Ellis, 2006, Art by Darryl Banks.

▲ If your story deals with space travel and technology, you should make sure your research provides you with enough details to make it all seem real.

Research: Veracity Is Everything

For an audience to believe in a writer's fictional world, the devil is always in the details. Connecting dozens of those details like pieces of a jigsaw puzzle to form a final, cohesive picture is your goal. Assuming you know the kind of story you want to tell and the genre in which it is placed, then the research to lay the foundation to suspend the disbelief of the readership should be your first task. For example, if your novel has a science-fiction setting, you'll need grounding in basic scientific principles, especially when dealing with space travel or technology.

E-FACT

THE MUSEUM OF COMIC AND CARTOON ART (MOCCA) IS LOCATED AT 594 BROADWAY, SUITE 401, NEW YORK, NY 10012. THE WEB SITE IS **www.moccany.org/online.html**. THIS PLACE IS A COMIC LOVER'S DREAM, WITH ALMOST EVERY COMIC ART GENRE REPRESENTED: GRAPHIC NOVELS, ANIMATION, ANIME, CARTOONS, COMIC BOOKS, COMIC STRIPS, GAG CARTOONS, EDITORIAL CARTOONS, ETC. CALL 212-254-3511 FOR MUSEUM HOURS.

Using the Internet

The Internet is an important resource for writers and artists alike. You can consult online dictionaries and encyclopedias, take virtual tours of museums and research the market for your book.

Check out these helpful links:

- The Comic Book Writer's Guide to Information on the Internet: **http://members.aol.com/jayjay5000/ WritersGuide.index.html**
- Comic Book Resources Forums: **http://forums.comicbookresources.com**
- Tools for Comics Creators: **www.hoboes.com/html/Comics/Creators**
- Artbomb.net: A Graphic Novel Explosion: **www.artbomb.net/home.jsp**
- Creative Markets: **www.hoboes.com/html/Comics/Creators/ Markets.html**

Image © Mark Ellis, 2006, Art by Darryl Banks.

⚠ Thoroughly research the time period in which you set your story—don't give a nineteenth-century character an automatic pistol when revolvers were in use.

The Background Setting

Establishing a believable backdrop for your graphic novel is the result of research. Even fantasy stories need to be believable within context. There are always details that need to seem real, whether they're weapons or eating utensils. J. R. R. Tolkien created very involved customs and traditions in his Middle-Earth saga, from the shape of the houses in Hobbiton to the types of clothes favored by the elves.

Basing a fantasy world on ancient Earth cultures is an accepted practice. Master fantasy writers Robert E. Howard and Fritz Leiber used everything from ancient Greece to Medieval Europe as templates for their fantasy universes.

E-FACT

JIMMY CORRIGAN, THE SMARTEST KID ON EARTH WAS CALLED "THE FIRST FORMAL MASTERPIECE OF THE MEDIUM." THIS COMIC APPEARED IN THE OCTOBER 1, 2005, ISSUE OF THE NEW YORKER. JIMMY IS PRESENTED AS AN UNHAPPY, LONELY MAN WHO ESCAPES HIS DRAB EXISTENCE THROUGH A RICH FANTASY LIFE.

If you're writing a period piece set in the Old West, be sure to thoroughly research the kind of firearms in use during that time. You don't want to give Wyatt Earp an automatic pistol, unless you're writing a time-travel tale.

Character Research

If you're using a historical personage as a major character in your story, research everything about that character. In *The Road to Perdition*, the award-winning graphic novel by Max Allan Collins, Frank Nitti, the number-two man of gangster Al Capone, played a pivotal role.

Frank Nitti was also an important character in Brian DePalma's film, *The Untouchables*, the story of Eliot Ness and his investigators battling the Capone mob in 1930s Chicago. In the last few minutes of the film, the audience watched Ness pursue and kill Nitti by throwing him from a rooftop.

In reality, Nitti lived for another decade and took his own life. The storytellers decided to sacrifice the historical reality for the sake of a plot point. *The Road to Perdition* presented a much more realistically drawn Frank Nitti.

The Current Market

Another important area to research is the market for your graphic novel. Thoroughly explore it; look at what is popular among readers and what the publishers are producing, then gauge what trends seem to be selling better than others. Where does your property fit in today's market? Also take note of the packaging, cover design, and title logo designs.

▼ A graphic novel featuring a serious treatment of real people such as gangster Frank Nitti should avoid the stereotypical view.

Image © Mark Ellis, 2006, Art by Don Heck.

Financial Resources and Commitment

Eventually in every creative endeavor the topic of costs rears its ugly head. If you feel that your concept and ideas are unique enough to be commercial and that you have the enthusiasm to carry through with all the steps necessary to complete the project, there are some facts that you should consider. First, printing costs have continued to increase over the last decade, and the cost of producing your graphic novel must be evaluated realistically.

E-SSENTIAL

ART SPIEGELMAN'S GRAPHIC NOVEL *MAUS* DEPICTED HIS JEWISH FAMILY'S ORDEAL UNDER THE NAZIS DURING THE HOLOCAUST AND WON THE PULITZER PRIZE IN 1986. THE 1992 PULITZER PRIZE BOARD CREATED A SPECIAL CATEGORY TO HONOR SPIEGELMAN AND THE STORY'S TWO VOLUMES, *MAUS I: A SURVIVOR'S TALE* AND *MAUS II: AND HERE MY TROUBLES BEGIN.*

▶ Before entering into a partnership with others to produce your graphic novel, make sure you're all on the same page.

Image © Mark Ellis, 2006, Art by Eddy Newell.

Next, you need to know a little about the prepress production to assess what a project will cost and what your profit will be. (Chapter 7 covers the various production steps involved for a graphic novel, from script to coloring.) Some creator-owned properties are produced as solo efforts, as in the case of Frank Miller, Mike Mignola, Art Spiegelman, and John Byrne, but more are produced as a collaboration between several creators, usually a writer and an artist, like Richard and Wendy Pini, or Jerry Siegel and Joe Shuster.

Obviously, the fewer people involved in the project, the less the profits will have to be split, but conversely, if more people are involved, the production time and workload will be reduced as well.

If working with others, even close friends or family members, be sure to draw up an agreement in writing, before publishing, which spells out what everyone's role in the project is and what the compensation for their efforts will be. This will help avoid any disagreements at a later point. All parties to the agreement should sign it and retain a copy for their records.

If working alone, this of course will not be necessary. What will be required is a strong work ethic and a well thought out production schedule. Whether working alone or with others, a deep commitment to the novel and a strong work ethic are required to undertake a project of this complexity.

Writing, penciling, inking, coloring, and lettering a ninety-page graphic novel is not for the faint-hearted. If you feel that you are up for the challenge, here are some facts you should know:

- Research shows the average independent comic book costs anywhere from $400 to $800 per page to produce. This is before printing costs are factored in. A graphic novel should be at least ninety pages long.
- Have sufficient resources to carry you through, specifically six months to one year's expenses, if you're working on the book full time plus enough money to pay print production costs, promotional costs, and enough to hire a lawyer and accountant to take care of those pesky business details when setting up your business.
- Different business models apply to small, independent publishers versus big corporations. If they keep their page rates low, independent publishers make all their money on the back end of the project. Be sure any collaborators are aware of this fact from the beginning.

If you're a Renaissance man or woman and can write as well as draw, you're in luck. Your project may take longer to produce, but it will undeniably reflect your unique vision of the book and you can avoid the conflicts that sometimes arise among multiple creators. Best of all, all the profit and glory will be yours.

Attitude and Determination

If you have researched the preliminary information about the process of creating a graphic novel and the fire still burns in your heart for the project, congratulations: You may be the rare individual who has what it takes to succeed in the business of comics and publishing. If you have done your homework and considered the practical aspects of your project, you'll be well positioned to prepare yourself for the various hats you'll have to wear during the process.

Fame and Glory

It takes a lot of energy to keep the creative fires burning during production and the challenges you will face before you eventually see your name on the cover of your finished graphic novel. If your primary motivation for the project is the thought of celebrity and riches, this is the time to rethink your approach. But if your primary motivation is the simple burning need to tell your story, you stand a much better chance of weathering the storms that inevitably will arise.

The Miskatonic Project © 2006 Mark Ellis, art by Don Heck.

▲ Keeping your goal in mind through all the research and preparation can sometimes be difficult, but by understanding the process you'll run into fewer roadblocks.

Proper Preparation

An understanding of the process and realistic planning for the project will help you navigate through the many minefields that await the novice. This is not meant as discouragement; plenty of people with a dream have achieved their goals and seen their books in print. Most of these fortunate individuals have drawn up a plan and followed it step by step. It's not rocket science, and proper preparation will get you to your goal.

E-FACT

IN A BOLD MARKETING MOVE, HARLEQUIN ENTERPRISES PUBLISHES MANGA VERSIONS OF OVER 250 OF ITS TITLES IN JAPAN UNDER A LICENSING AGREEMENT WITH JAPAN'S OHZORA PUBLISHING COMPANY, A CREATOR OF MANGA TITLES. IN AN EAST-MEETS-WEST APPROACH, HARLEQUIN ROMANCE WRITERS ARE TEAMED WITH JAPANESE MANGA ARTISTS.

It Pays to Be Positive

If you have done your research, gathered your resources, and checked your motivations, feel confident in proceeding with your project. Ignore naysayers and snipers of negativity. There will always be those who can't achieve their own dreams and try to squash the dreams of others. Let those words roll off your back. A positive attitude at this stage is your greatest ally; it will see you through any minor setbacks.

Time Management

Entering the dangerous waters of time management is the bane of all creators, writers, and artists who may not have as rigid a standard in this regard as most people. From long experience, we have a few tips and suggestions to offer in this matter. Trying to juggle and balance everyday commitments from work to family often seems like a strenuous series of gymnastic tricks. Some may be obvious, but all bear mentioning.

Schedule Yourself

Although it is easier said than done, reserving a block of time per day or per week to work on your graphic novel is an essential first step. Treat this time as if you were at a regular job, resisting interruption wherever possible.

Some people balk at the very idea, but establishing a daily or weekly quota for yourself is one sure way of getting the job done. All too often the real world intrudes into your creativity, bringing on both frustration and conflict. This is the point where it is vital to remind yourself that you are the boss who set the quota and that you have to live up to the commitments you made to yourself and your goals.

Organization Is Your Friend

Getting organized doesn't always come naturally to creative people. Therefore, trying to organize time, material, and mindset on a schedule isn't easy, but it must be done.

Death Hawk and all characters © 2006 Mark Ellis, art by Darryl Banks.

▲ Establishing a daily or weekly quota toward completion of your graphic novel isn't always easy, but it is one sure way of getting the job done. Make sure to back up all your computer files.

Make a list of every possible step along the way that you may need to keep track of. Laying events and deadlines out in loose chronological order really helps in planning.

Keep your time management practical, realistic, and within the parameters of your personal situation at home or at work. Keep in mind that things always take a lot longer than you think they are going to. A large desk calendar and work flow chart will help keep you well organized as well as help you plan realistically and track vital deadlines.

A Rolodex or some other system for organizing contact information is vital. Microsoft Outlook and other organizational or project tracking software work quite well, too, as long as you regularly back up your computer files to a CD or flash drive. Few things are a bigger waste of time or more frustrating than losing your vital contact information.

Image © Mark Ellis 2006, art by Jim Mooney.

▲ You can gain a sense of satisfaction by reaching daily goals in the production of your graphic novel.

Eyes on the Prize

Set the goal you want to achieve every day you work on the graphic novel, but stay flexible—leave yourself and the project enough room to be retooled or reworked as new ideas or concepts occur to you. One of the few benefits of being your own boss is the ability to cut yourself some slack, but be sure this option doesn't become a regular habit. Striking a balance requires maturity and a sense of responsibility to yourself and others. There is a great sense of satisfaction to be gained as you see the project coming closer to fruition each day.

Contacts in the Industry

Not unlike the film industry, achieving success in the graphic novel field is often as much a matter of who you know as what you know. Making contacts in the comics arena isn't necessarily a prerequisite to success, but getting to know editors and other creators can help you reach your goal, and it can keep you in the creative loop and increase your odds of success.

Conventions

Attending large comics-oriented conventions such as the Atlanta Comic Convention, MegaCon in Orlando, the Big Apple Comic Con in NYC, and the San Diego Comic Con is a great way to meet fellow creators and industry professionals. But if you are too far from a big city or your budget does not permit the expense of travel and hotels, there may be a smaller convention nearby or in your region.

▼ Attending comics-oriented functions and conventions is a good way to meet other creators and even set up a fan base for yourself and your work.

The New Justice Machine © 2006 Mark Ellis, art by Darryl Banks.

Web sites such as **www.comicbookconventions.com/conventions.htm** and **http://comicon.com/index.html** are a great way of finding conventions near you.

Creator Signings

Scan the Internet and local papers as well as bulletin boards in bookstores and comic shops for book signings in your area. This is a great opportunity to network one-on-one and to get a chance to talk to an industry professional who just a few short years ago may have been where you are now. Don't try to show your portfolio at this time, but if you strike up a rapport, showing a few sketches might be in order.

Forums and Online Communities

While you're out there on the Web, check out the many online forums and message boards where you can interact with established professionals and other aspiring creators. These can prove to be an invaluable source of information and contacts. For example, check out **http://comicbooks.about.com/mpboards.htm**, **www.comixtreme.com/forums**, and **http://p.webring.com/hub?ring=cbartists**.

The Miskatonic Project © 2006 Mark Ellis, art by Darryl Banks.

▲ Showing sketches of your work in progress to an industry professional at a book signing or a convention is a good way to receive feedback.

CHAPTER 3

DEVELOPING THE CONCEPT

Every graphic novel requires an underlying concept, be it simple or complex. The concept is the basis of your story, and it is only limited by your own imagination and creative capacities. The concept may even have been done before, but if this is the case, it must be given a new twist on an old theme. It must be uniquely your own; its energy is what will drive the story and capture the imagination of your audience. You might even call it the heart of the novel.

The Plot

The plot, or the ordering of the events or actions in a story, may not be the most important element of your story, but it provides the framework on which to build your storyline as well as your characters. Plots can be driven by a conflict, such as man versus nature, man versus society, or man versus himself—or a combination of the three.

You don't need much to base a plot on conflicts or struggles. The plot of the *Star Wars* saga stems from these three basic conflicts, as does Will Eisner's *A Contract with God*.

Although the novel is semiautobiographical, with Eisner drawing on his own childhood experiences growing up in the Bronx, the conflicts are fundamentally the same as those in *Star Wars*. In this work, plot and character are tightly intertwined.

V for Vendetta, by Alan Moore and David Lloyd, is a complex tale told from several different viewpoints. Relying heavily on symbolism, it still depicts variations of the three main conflicts.

Characters, their interactions and their conflicts, should be structured to drive the plot toward the heart of your story.

▶ Jason Redquill, aka Lakota, must deal with different conflicts in his life, the main one being the beautiful but dangerous Catamount.

Lakota and all characters © 2006 Mark Ellis, art by Jim Mooney.

Death Hawk and all characters © 2006 Mark Ellis, art by Adam Hughes.

△ Death Hawk and con woman Vanessa Bouvier share an intimate moment.

Granted not all plots need to be about physical struggles, but since the graphic narrative form is far more visual than cerebral, you will have to depend on the strength of the artwork to carry the reader through your novel.

In *Lakota*, Jason Redquill grapples with coming to terms with his role as a warrior-shaman while he tries to function as a modern academic. Without his internal and external conflicts, the plot could not move forward, nor could he interact with the other main characters, such as his mentor Tall Bull and the seductive Catamount. Even so, much of the conflict is presented as a series of physical confrontations.

E-FACT

MARJANE SATRAPI'S GRAPHIC NOVEL *PERSEPOLIS*, A STORY SET DURING THE IRANIAN REVOLUTION, IS REQUIRED READING AT WEST POINT. THE TEACHERS HOPE IT WILL GIVE CADETS A BETTER RESOURCE FOR UNDERSTANDING THE CULTURE THAN NEWSPAPERS, TEXTS, OR STUDIES COULD PROVIDE.

The ultrarealistic (or slice of life) approach has worked well with such graphic novels as *Ghost World* and *Art School Confidential*, where the actual plot parameters are vaguely defined but are still influenced by aspects of man versus society and man versus himself.

Subplots can be woven throughout the story, either by the introduction of characters or secondary elements that then turn out to be of great importance to the overall plot. In *Death Hawk: The Soulworm Saga*, the search for alien artifacts turns into an unexpected quest for spiritual transformation on the part of con woman Vanessa Bouvier. In this, despite the space-opera treasure hunt, the plot depends on basic human values.

E-FACT

EVEN THOUGH COMIC BOOK SALES HAVE DECLINED OVER THE YEARS, BOOKSELLERS IN AMERICA AND EUROPE SAY GRAPHIC NOVELS ARE AMONG THEIR FASTEST GROWING CATEGORIES. IN **2004**, BORDERS, ONE OF AMERICA'S LARGEST BOOKSTORE CHAINS, ANNOUNCED GRAPHIC NOVEL SALES HAD RISEN MORE THAN **100** PERCENT A YEAR FOR THE PRECEDING THREE YEARS.

Keep in mind that although it's possible to create a graphic novel that is very light on plot and driven more by character interaction, readers may not enjoy reading a plotless story unless your characters are very strong and memorable.

Conversely, you don't have to break your brain to come up with an original plot. Execution, how your story is presented to the reader, is the important thing. The plot may be old, but the manner in which your novel is written can make it seem fresh and new. Just don't follow a formula and make it too predictable.

Cast of Characters

The linchpins of any story are the characters. Although a plot may grow from a convincing cast, only rarely can a plot in and of itself produce convincing characters. A wonderfully innovative plot can be undercut and nullified by weak characterization, and this is especially true in a visual medium like graphic novels.

Characters in conventional prose novels should be memorable, but in graphic novels they must be larger than life, both in mannerism and appearance. They should be as unique as you can make them instead of embodying a laundry list of pop culture clichés. Ideally your cast should transcend the limitations of a single plot, even if your story and your characters are inextricably linked.

E-FACT

COMICS SCRIPTER ALAN MOORE EXPANDED UPON THE POST-WONDERLAND ADVENTURES OF LEWIS CARROLL'S ALICE IN HIS MATURE-THEMED GRAPHIC NOVEL *THE LOST GIRLS*, IN WHICH THE GROWNUP ALICE COMES TO TERMS WITH HER PAST HELPED BY WENDY DARLING OF JAMES BARRIE'S *PETER PAN*.

Death Hawk and all characters © 2006 Mark Ellis, art by Adam Hughes.

WHAT'D HE SAY?

HELIGSON OR THE SIKHIAN?

SPUDS LIGHT

WHO DO *YOU* THINK?

🔺 The interplay between Death Hawk and his protosymbiotic partner, Cyke, developed both characters and advanced the plot.

Even if your novel is about a single central character, you will still need a cast of allies and adversaries for him to interact with. For example, Bob Kane realized early on that Batman needed someone to talk to and bounce ideas off of and thus came Robin, whose introduction made Batman less fearsome but more human.

Sherlock Holmes has Dr. Watson, and in comics Superman has Lois Lane. The interaction with other people humanized both characters. Secondary players (often known as "second bananas") are important to add complexity and tone. Your hero can say or do something and his friend/sidekick can either argue or point out something that has been overlooked. It adds a slightly different focus, which can move the plot of your story forward.

In *Death Hawk: The Soulworm Saga*, the two primary protagonists are a twenty-fifth century salvage expert and his partner, an artificial life form named Cyke. The creature is telepathic and possesses several psychic abilities, hence his name, a pun on *psych*. Not only is he extremely intelligent, Cyke is often more knowledgeable about most things than his human partner, and he isn't above rubbing Death Hawk's nose in this fact.

Death Hawk and all characters © 2006 Mark Ellis, art by Adam Hughes.

IN SOME UNKNOWN MANNER, IT APPEARS MS. BOUVIER HAS... *ABSORBED* THE PROPERTIES OF THE ARTIFACT—

IN ESSENCE, SHE *IS* THE ARTIFACT.

WHAT?!!

◀ Cyke lets Death Hawk in on a secret concerning their guest, Vanessa.

▶ In comics, attitude and personality can often be established through exaggeration.

Paladin Alpha © 2006 Mark Ellis, art by Matt Roberts.

Ideally you want to create characters who seem to come to life on their own without providing a great deal of supplemental information. However, this often proves elusive, hence the preponderance of origin stories that can be found for most comic book heroes out there in the market.

▼ The very first appearance of Jason Redquill in *Lakota* displays much about him as a character.

Lakota © 2006 Mark Ellis, art by Jim Mooney.

In *Lakota*, Jason Redquill enters the scene complete and fully formed. The reader isn't sure of who he is, what he is, or how he came to be, even though several hints are dropped throughout the first section of the story.

Regardless of history or origin story, stereotypical characters or standard-issue imitations of well-known characters won't engender much in the way of reader interest. There is little reason for a reader to care about copies when stories about the originals are available.

The New Justice Machine © 2006 Mark Ellis, art by Darryl Banks.

Caricatures are a different matter. Since this is a visual medium, portraying characters with big heads, lantern jaws, or scarred faces is part and parcel of the form. Exaggeration is the norm, not the exception.

Setting and Timeline

Although the setting of your graphic novel is somewhat secondary to plot and characterization, it is nevertheless an integral element that has a great deal of impact on all other aspects of the book. It is the stage on which your characters play out the story, and in order for the action to be believable, the reader must buy that the setting is indeed a real place, even if it exists only in your imagination. A powerful enough setting can become a character in its own right, like Batman's Gotham City.

The advantage of anchoring your novel in a real place is that your reader will already be grounded in reality. One of the reasons for the popularity of Marvel Comics in the 1960s was the use of New York City as a setting rather than a fictitious place such as Metropolis.

◀ The planet Sikh is established as a setting before the action begins in *Death Hawk: The Soulworm Saga*.

Familiar Manhattan landmarks such as the Empire State Building or Radio City Music Hall added an air of verisimilitude to the adventures of Spider-Man and the Fantastic Four. Mood and atmosphere are greatly enhanced by a believable setting, particularly if your story is science fiction or has supernatural trappings.

When the setting is introduced, it draws the reader into the scene and orients them as to time and geography, more so if the scene is exotic in some way. *Death Hawk: The Soulworm Saga* introduces the setting of the planet Sikh before any of the characters are onstage.

If you place your story in the past, to make it seem real you'll have to do a great deal of research. The graphic novel *The Whisperer in Darkness*, set in 1928, required artist Don Heck to consult period reference material depicting cars, fashions, and even small details like wristwatches.

A story set in nineteenth-century Washington, D.C., certainly shouldn't show automobiles driving up and down Pennsylvania Avenue or show the grounds of the White House ringed by protective walls—they simply weren't there in that era.

The Miskatonic Project © 2006 Mark Ellis, art by Don Heck.

▲ From *The Miskatonic Project*: a street scene in 1928 New York, beautifully detailed by artist Don Heck.

Image © 2006 Mark Ellis, art by Darryl Banks.

Death Hawk and all characters © 2006 Mark Ellis, art by Rik Levins.

🔺 The White House in 1876 was considerably different in appearance than it was in the twentieth century.

🔺 The top three panels of this page bring the reader up-to-date by relating the high points of the previous chapter in *Death Hawk: The Soulworm Saga*.

Establishing a timeline is also an important element of your novel. The passage of time within the story shapes the characters and the plot. Graphic novels, being primarily a visual medium, should have a fast, strong opening and decelerate after the setting, characters, and basics of the plot are introduced.

You can vary the speed of the narrative when new characters and concepts come on-stage, but developing scenes and building the drama depends on how your story is paced. The simplest way to deal with time is to follow action linearly from beginning to end.

You could also start the story in the middle of a conflict and then show the events that led up to the point where the story began through a series of flashbacks.

Placing the events of your story in a straightforward sequence has the advantage of showing cause and effect, going from point A to point B, but that also commits you to following what you have already established in regards to plot and character.

Conversely, by starting somewhere in the middle of the story and dropping background information in small hints, your readers draw inferences and conclusions for themselves, yet you won't necessarily be constrained to follow their interpretations. That leaves you the element of surprise, and you can maintain suspense and reader excitement by doing the unexpected.

Research Methods

Once you decide what your graphic novel is all about, both the writer and artist will need reference materials, the groundwork of your novel. The artist will need a *clip file*, which contains photographs, artwork, and anything else pertaining to setting or props, from guns to shoes.

Some artists, like the legendary Jack Kirby and the equally legendary Jim Mooney, could draw entire armies and cities from memory. However, artists of this caliber are few and far between. Most artists collect extensive clip (or swipe) files with examples of anything that might be needed.

E-ALERT

ON THE FIRST SATURDAY IN MAY, PARTICIPATING COMIC RETAILERS ACROSS THE COUNTRY OFFER FREE PROMOTIONAL COMIC BOOKS TO ATTRACT NEW READERS INTO THEIR SHOPS. THE MAJOR PUBLISHERS OFFER A COMIC THAT THEY BELIEVE WILL MOST LIKELY ATTRACT NEW NONCOMIC READERS. CALLED FREE COMIC BOOK DAY, THE PRACTICE STARTED IN **2002.**

Many of today's comics artists like to pay homage to their own favorite artists or use certain images or models for inspiration, so they compile their own swipe files of stock character poses, facial expressions, and even perspectives. Famed paperback cover artist Robert McGuinness is credited with saying, "An artist is only as good as his clip file."

In portraying place and objects accurately, both the artist and writer must pay attention to authenticity, and that requires diligent research. Even if the setting is imaginary, you should strive to make it seem as real as possible with a degree of believable consistency in everything that appears in the novel.

The New Justice Machine © 2006 Mark Ellis, art by Darryl Banks.

🔺 The design of Death Hawk's ship, the Peregrine, suggested that it actually could operate in deep space.

E-FACT

GRAPHIC LITERATURE MAY HAVE FINALLY BROKEN OUT OF SPECIALTY STORES AND INTO THE MAIN-STREAM TO GET THE RESPECT IT DESERVES, AND IT NOW PRODUCES STORIES THAT ARE MORE TRUE TO REAL-LIFE THEMES. PROFESSORS IN THE UNITED STATES AND EUROPE ARE OFFERING COMICS-BASED LITERATURE CLASSES IN UNIVERSITIES AND COLLEGES. IN FRANCE, THE MINISTER OF CULTURE PRESIDED OVER THE FIRST NATIONAL CELEBRATION OF COMIC ART IN 2004 AND EVEN KNIGHTED ART-ISTS FROM BELGIUM, JAPAN, AND FRANCE.

For writers, finding references is a bit tougher, particularly if you're writing science fiction and want to maintain plausibility. There are several Web sites that can be consulted for science fiction research, including the Hard Science Sites for Science Fiction Author Research at *www.computercrowsnest.com/directory/fdscint.php*.

If you believe in the world you create, more than likely your audience will as well. Good research is the foundation of your fictional universe.

CHAPTER 4

GENRES GALORE

The easiest thing for writers or artists to choose is the genre in which they want to work. However, having a basic grasp of the different categories and their strengths and weaknesses should be part of the decision-making process. There are many reasons to choose one genre or subgenre over the other, but your choice should be the one you feel the most enthusiastic about. This chapter examines the six most popular genres in the graphic novel field and evaluates what is best and worst about them.

Superheroes

Superheroes and the graphic novel go together like the proverbial horse and carriage. The superhero concept has been synonymous with comic books for nearly seventy years. In the 1930s and throughout the '40s, the super-hero represented the best of humanity. Supervillains were rare in early comic books, but corruption in high and low places was commonplace. Evil mayors, police commissioners on the take, and Nazis were the primary adversaries of the superhero.

One of the first and longest-lived approaches in the genre was to combine superheroes into a team, like the Justice League of America and the Avengers. As time went on, the team premise turned into the superfamily, represented first by the Fantastic Four then later by the X-Men.

Paladin Alpha © 2006 Mark Ellis, art by Matt Roberts.

▲ Flight and the ability to hurl energy bolts—but super powers don't always make the hero.

In *Paladin Alpha: Hellfire Trigger*, the super-hero character is the last survivor of what was once a superteam of the future, the Paladins Prime. The first chapter depicts Paladin Alpha's final battle with his arch foe, Lord Rogue. Paladin Alpha is hurled back in time and becomes an amnesiac. He learns who he is and how he came to be at the same time as the reader does, discovering his link with the mysterious Quantum Gauntlet.

In *The Justice Machine: The Chimera Conspiracy*, a superteam family struggles to maintain some semblance of normalcy while battling their opposite numbers, Department Z, and dealing with the return of an old foe in a new guise, the evil Darkforce. Stories about superheroes by their very nature are larger than life. They feature extreme characters, situations, and even facial expressions. Almost nothing appears in normal human scale.

The New Justice Machine and Department Z © Mark Ellis, 2006, art by Darryl Banks.

▲ One of the conventions of a superteam story is that they must face an enemy superteam, demonstrated here by the Justice Machine versus Department Z.

◀ In the superhero tale, everything is exaggerated, even facial expressions.

Paladin Alpha © 2006 Mark Ellis, art by Matt Roberts.

▼ Chaotic fight scenes in superhero tales are part and parcel of the genre.

Costumes that convey a sense of the characters' extraordinary abilities yet don't look ridiculous can be difficult to carry off artistically. In fight scenes featuring two opposing superteams, chaos must be suggested without the scene actually becoming chaotic. Readers should be able to follow the action without confusion.

IN MY BOOK, JACK, YOU'RE JUST A *DRIP!*

GASP

The New Justice Machine © 2006 Mark Ellis, art by Darryl Banks.

The biggest problem facing graphic novel creators who want to work in the genre is the competition. Both DC and Marvel pump out an enormous amount of product featuring well-known characters like Superman, Batman, and Spider-Man. Your own unique character can be done, but only by discarding the standard formula of a teenaged superhero who encounters problems juggling homework with his world-saving career. Strive for originality. Although working in the superhero genre is very appealing and a lot of fun, the realities of the competition should be seriously researched before starting your book.

The Crime Genre

The crime genre is one of the most popular in the graphic novel field. *Crime Does Not Pay*, the first of the so-called crime comics, appeared in 1942. Controversial from the beginning, but also very popular, it was imitated by many publishers with titles like *Shock Suspense Stories* and *Trapped!* Although *Crime Does Not Pay* usually featured fact-based but exaggerated accounts of criminals colliding with law enforcement, it rarely glamorized the gangsters.

By the 1990s, the crime comic was back in favor, showcased by graphic novels such as *Sin City*, *The Road to Perdition*, and *A History of Violence*. Written by John Wagner and illustrated by Vince Locke, *A History of Violence* concerns a small-town restaurant owner who becomes a local hero after foiling a robbery in his cafe.

When the news report of the incident gains national attention, several members of the New York mob arrive in town to exact vengeance against the man for crossing them decades before.

E-FACT

CRIME DOES NOT PAY ENJOYED ENORMOUS POPULARITY AND REACHED ITS PEAK OF SALES IN 1947 WHEN IT BOASTED A CIRCULATION OF OVER SEVEN MILLION, MORE THAN THE AGGREGATE SALES OF ALL COMIC BOOKS SOLD IN THE DIRECT MARKET IN 2005, ACCORDING TO DIAMOND COMIC DISTRIBUTORS.

Road to Perdition, by Max Allan Collins and Richard Piers Payner, deals much more straightforwardly with organized crime. When the story's protagonist, a Chicago hit man, finds that his wife and small daughter have been gunned down by a man he trusted, he and his young son set out on a path to find justice.

Sin City is much more fantasy-like, inspired by Frank Miller's fondness for film noir gangster films and 1950s paperbacks that featured hard-boiled protagonists. Sin City itself is a fictional town in the Northwest plagued by an astronomical crime rate, serial killers, and a corrupt police force. It is like Gotham City but without Batman to act as a mitigating influence on the underworld.

Because of the adult themes of most crime stories, graphic novels are perfectly suited for portraying vicious gangsters and all manner of criminal activities. Violence, sexuality, and profanity are accepted as appropriate in this genre.

E-SSENTIAL

IN 1976, JIM STERANKO WROTE AND ILLUSTRATED *CHANDLER: RED TIDE*, A 130-PAGE GRAPHIC NOVEL THAT IS GENERALLY CONSIDERED THE FIRST POST-SILVER AGE CRIME COMIC. BECAUSE IT DIDN'T HAVE WORD BALLOONS OR CAPTIONS, IT WAS NOT WIDELY EMBRACED BY THE COMIC BOOK COMMUNITY.

Although the crime genre isn't as competitive as the superhero genre, the creators of graphic novels focusing on crime should find a unique twist and avoid the clichés of rat-faced informants and pinstriped racketeers. Still, hard-boiled tales influenced by film noir remain popular.

Science Fiction and Fantasy

Fantasy and science fiction are often lumped together as a single genre, although there are distinct differences between the two. They are best summed up by this statement: Science fiction can possibly happen and sometimes shouldn't, but fantasy can't possibly happen but should. Both rely on imagination, but science fiction is rooted in some form of fact, even speculative, while in fantasy anything is possible.

Image © 2006 Mark Ellis, art by Scott Benefiel.

▲ Crime stories featuring hard-boiled gangsters never go out of style.

There are many subgenres of science fiction to explore, from cyberpunk to postapocalyptic, although the most enduring is still space opera. That is the umbrella designation for everything from *Star Trek* to *Stargate SG-1*. Space opera deals with the exploration of alien planets or is set in a future when such things have long been established.

However, there is quite a bit of cross-pollination among the science fiction subgenres. Graphic novels featuring futuristic wars, known as military sci-fi, very often borrow from the cyberpunk and psychological subgenres.

Death Hawk: The Soulworm Saga is set in the late twenty-fifth century when interstellar travel and relations with extraterrestrial races are facts of life. But unlike *Star Trek*, it presents a future that is grim and dystopian. Anyone who is respectable must work for one of the many solar-system-spanning corporations that hold the true reins of power in the Sol 9 Commonwealth.

The protagonist is a freelance salvage expert who, with his protosymbiote partner, Cyke, operates on the rim of the civilized worlds, piloting his fifty-year-old ship, the *Peregrine*. They become involved in a quest to recover artifacts from the long-dead Skril race and in the process are caught up in many intrigues.

Elements of the Indiana Jones films as well as *The Treasure of the Sierra Madre* are suggested in the storyline. However, the science-fictional trappings in the graphic novel are based on actual scientific principles.

Death Hawk and Cyke © 2006 Mark Ellis, art by Darryl Banks.

△ Death Hawk and his partner Cyke operate a salvage business, a dangerous occupation in the twenty-fifth century.

Death Hawk and all characters © 2006 Mark Ellis, art by Rik Levins.

△ Making imaginative elements seem real is very important in a science-fiction setting.

Just as there are subgenres of science fiction, there are fantasy subgenres, which allow for the crossover of horror elements and romance. Epic fantasy can be defined by J. R. R. Tolkien's *Lord of the Rings* trilogy, featuring the world of Middle Earth where folkloric creatures, from elves to trolls, interact regularly. Role-playing games like Dungeons & Dragons have made epic fantasy part of the cultural landscape.

▲ In fantasy, magic and magic users abound, from warlocks to beautiful sorceresses.

Sword and sorcery, as exemplified by Robert E. Howard's Conan stories, combines myth and thinly veiled history with horror. As with epic fantasy, magic takes the place of science, and evil wizards, sword-wielding warriors, and beautiful sorceresses populate these stories. Fantasy is an attractive genre, since the stories can take place in any time and on any world. *Elfquest* and *A Distant Soil* are two successes in this graphic novel field.

The Horror Genre

Ironically, comic books like *Tales from the Crypt*, *The Vault of Horror*, and *The Haunt of Fear* are held partially responsible for the decline of the industry in the 1950s when horror, like crime comics, fell on very hard times. It wasn't until 1965 and the first issue of *Creepy* that horror bounced back. When the strictures of the Comics Code were loosened, tales of vampires, werewolves, walking mummies, and zombies were once again featured in the graphic narrative.

E-FACT

E.C., THE PUBLISHER AGAINST WHICH THE COMICS CODE AUTHORITY'S RULES WERE THE MOST RESTRICTIVE, CANCELLED THEIR HORROR COMICS AND CAME OUT WITH WAR COMICS ENTITLED *VALOR* AND *ACES HIGH* AND TWO ODDBALL ENTRIES, *M.D.* AND *PSYCHOANALYSIS*, ABOUT THE MEDICAL PROFESSION. NONE OF THESE COMICS WERE AS SUCCESSFUL AS THEIR HORROR TITLES.

However, since 1965 the horror genre has come a very long way from tales of vampires, werewolves, and ghosts. Although versions of Dracula and Frankenstein remain popular, many of the conventions established in those seminal works are now considered passé.

The elegant, cultured vampires of Anne Rice supplanted the mindless blood-lusting fiends of an earlier day. Vampires who wore ruffled shirts and played the violin became the standard version of the children of the night.

However, the approach taken in *Nosferatu: Plague of Terror* was to return to an earlier folkloric incarnation of the vampire. Based loosely on the silent film *Nosferatu: A Symphony of Terror*, it went back to the roots of the vampire legend, depicting vampires as creatures of filth and disease.

In this reworking of the classic tale, Baron Graf Orlock matches wits with Sir William Longsword, a knight he has cursed with immortality who pursues him through history as Orlock perpetuates evil. Their final confrontation takes place in an abandoned church in the Bronx with an army of plague-infected rats preparing to swarm the city. Both Orlock and Longsword perish, but not before the curse of the Nosferatu is passed on to an innocent bystander.

Horror works well in combination with other genres, such as mystery and even fantasy, but the overall goal should be to frighten and unnerve the reader.

▶ In folklore, vampires were never portrayed as charming or cultured but as harbingers of disease.

Nosferatu: Plague of Terror © 2006 Mark Ellis, art by Richard Pace.

As an example of cross-genre storytelling, *The Whisperer in Darkness* featured the Miskatonic Project, a group of paranormal investigators facing the Great Old Ones, monsters created by legendary horror writer, H. P. Lovecraft. Functioning as a sort of Depression-era *X-Files*, the Project tracks down the extraterrestrial Mi-Go and destroys their brain-harvesting operation. The story borrows elements from science fiction as well as from hard-boiled detective yarns.

▶ Intelligent monsters such as the Mi-Go made for frightening adversaries in *The Whisperer in Darkness* graphic novel.

The Miskatonic Project © Mark Ellis 2006, art by Don Heck.

RUSTLE SKRASH SKRUNCH RUSTLE

-- IN OVER SEVENTY MILLION YEARS.

RHIIISSSSSSS

Explorers © Terry Collins and Bill Neville 2006, art by Bill Neville.

◄ In *Explorers*, Dr. Hunt and his family travel the globe facing the fantastic and the unknown.

Most graphic novels in this genre tend to be bloody and violent, as well as contain sexual situations. Whatever approach you take with your horror tale, keep in mind that your ultimate goal is to frighten an audience, not gross them out.

The Adventure Genre

This is the most wide open of all genres, since aspects of so many others can be seamlessly grafted onto it. Spies, archeologists, soldiers of fortune, and femme fatales can race from one peril to another and encounter the supernatural and the science-fictional along the way.

James Bond and Indiana Jones films and television series like *Lost* follow the adventure genre blueprint, regardless of the introduction of elements from other categories.

Adventure is the one genre that is always durable and never truly goes out of style. It is also flexible and allows for many different types of stories to be told. Adventure tales can take place in the future, the past, or in contemporary times.

The milestone adventure series told in the graphic narrative format is Milton Caniff's *Terry and the Pirates*. For nearly seventy years it has been held as the standard by which almost all adventure comics are judged.

Originally set in 1930s China, *Terry* established the model of resourceful explorers in exotic atmospheres with jungles, ancient temples, planes, and boats as the visual backdrops. Caniff is regarded as one of the masters of the graphic narrative. *Terry and the Pirates*, as well as his later *Steve Canyon* strip, were often imitated but never surpassed. His work provided inspiration for cartoonists, writers, and even filmmakers. His creation, Lai Choi San, the Dragon Lady, became a cultural icon.

E-FACT

MILTON CANIFF RECALLED THAT WHEN HE PUT TOGETHER THE ELEMENTS OF WHAT WOULD BECOME *TERRY AND THE PIRATES*, HE SUBMITTED A LIST OF NAMES FOR THE MAIN CHARACTER TO THE EDITOR OF THE TIMES-NEWS SYNDICATE. THE EDITOR CIRCLED TERRY AND WROTE "AND THE PIRATES" BESIDE IT.

One of the most enduring themes in all of literature is that of the explorer, the stranger in the strange land. This concept was reinvented for new audiences by Terry Collins and Bill Neville with *Explorers*. Dr. Alexander Hunt and his family are Xenology, Inc., a scientific team whose explorations take them into ancient Mayan pyramids and even lost worlds populated by dinosaurs.

Biographical Works

There are two types of biographies in the graphic novel field. One deals with the lives of public figures like Malcolm X and even NASCAR drivers. The other, known as autobio, details the life stories of the authors of the work and is more prevalent in today's market.

Autobio became popular in the underground comics' movement of the 1960s and over the years was accepted by the mainstream. These graphic novels are usually stories of relationships, personal tragedies, and even comedy.

Japanese artist/writer Keji Nakazawa told of his firsthand experience following the bombing of Hiroshima, and the basic story of *Barefoot Gen* was later adapted into three films. Harvey Pekar's *American Splendor* began in 1976 and detailed his life as a file clerk in a Cleveland Hospital. Many of the stories were adapted in the 2004 film of the same title.

Perhaps the best known entry in the autobio genre is Art Spiegelman's Pulitzer Prize–winning *Maus*, which detailed his father's experience in a concentration camp during World War II and Spiegelman's relationship with his father. This work had a major positive impact on the general public's perception of comics.

Autobio obviously doesn't require a great deal of research, but the creators should be careful about the kind of stories they want to tell. Unless there is a very unusual twist or wrinkle to the tale, the audience for an angst-filled memoir of life in junior high school will

Image © 2006 Mark Ellis, art by Don Hillsman.

◀ The life of civil rights activist Malcolm X was the subject of a graphic novel in the early 1990s.

be limited. The creators also should be aware of the legalities involved in using the likenesses of real people without their permission.

Biographical comics are often intended as an educational tool, since they encapsulate the lives of historical figures or events. In this form, an exceptional degree of research is necessary. Throughout the 1960s, biographical comics were a very popular genre. DC published *Bible Stories*, and Dell had an entire line that included the life stories of Dwight D.

Eisenhower, Adlai Stevenson, and even the Beatles.

Beginning in the 1990s, several independent publishers revived the concept with celebrity and personality comics imprints. These focused mainly on unauthorized biographies of actors and rock stars. A few companies still publish biographical comics for specialized readerships, particularly for young people who belong to various religious denominations.

Although graphic novels in either the autobio or biographical forms have proven track records, the market for them is probably the most uncertain of all the genres. They should be approached carefully, after diligent research and study.

CHAPTER 5

WRITING THE SCRIPT

Writing a script for a graphic novel is a far different discipline than writing straight prose. It can be challenging, which is often a euphemism for difficult, and there are certain rules that must be followed. Writing a graphic novel requires you to think visually, and you need to communicate those visuals to an artist. The process is not as easy as you might think, but with practice you can make rapid progress.

Visual Storytelling and the Story Arc

Even if you're working as both artist and writer, when you begin to write the script, you'll to need to compose the images as a series of panels and present them in a way that the reader can easily follow. Unlike a prose novelist, the graphic novel writer is removing the middle man, the reader's imagination. A novelist uses words to describe a character and a setting, relying on the reader's imagination to conjure up mental images. Graphic novels take away all of that, showing the reader rather than telling. The fiction writer's dictum of "show, don't tell" is nowhere more in force than in comics scripting. You don't have to tell the reader what an old mansion looks like. The artist provides that from the shutters hanging askew to the bats fluttering around the belfry.

However, you should understand from the outset that you'll be using a form of visual short-hand. If you wrote a prose story, you would describe the characters' actions as a step-by-step progression. For example, in a novel you would write, "Lord Sabbath, annoyed by Baron Morcar's impertinent question, only glared in response."

By employing the graphic narrative form, the exposition is replaced by a single panel of a close-up of Lord Sabbath giving the off-panel Baron Morcar an icy stare.

If the artist understands the mood of a scene, there is no need for any descriptive adjectives. The panel can be wordless yet still convey all the emotional nuance of exposition. Since it's easier for our minds to process images than text, the old proverb about a single picture being worth a thousand words is particularly appropriate in this instance.

▶ *Lord Sabbath, Duelist.*

© 2006 Mark Ellis, art by Shawn Budd.

Visual storytelling is less an art than a technique, and it's difficult for even an accomplished scriptwriter to master. When you write, every page must continue the thread of the story, so the progression of panels shouldn't be just a series of static images. You have to keep in mind that the art itself is the catalyst for the story arc; it's the vehicle for the finished product. Keep it moving; actions speak louder than words. Every page should be a self-contained unit, almost a minichapter within the larger work. The last panel on every page should contain a small *kicker*, something that motivates the reader to turn to the next page.

Script Versus Breakdowns

There are several different approaches to creating the script for your graphic novel. The most common one is to use the method known as *full script*. This form works best if the writer is working with an artist, dividing the labor.

A full script is laid out essentially like a screen or teleplay, with all the dialogue complete and all the action described and blocked out in panels. The writer provides both the instruction and stage direction, describing physical appearances of various characters and objects and often suggesting panel composition. Even when working alone, this technique is very helpful.

E-FACT

LEGENDARY MOVIE DIRECTOR ORSON WELLES WAS A VERY BIG FAN OF COMICS, EVEN APPLYING LIGHTING TECHNIQUES AND CAMERA ANGLES INSPIRED BY *BATMAN* TO HIS MAGNUM OPUS, *CITIZEN KANE*. ACCORDING TO RECENT RUMORS, WELLES SERIOUSLY CONSIDERED MAKING A BATMAN MOVIE AS EARLY AS 1946 AND WENT SO FAR AS PRODUCING PRODUCTION DESIGNS, AN EARLY DRAFT OF A SCRIPT, AND SOME CASTING PHOTOGRAPHS FEATURING PROTOTYPES OF WHAT WOULD EVENTUALLY BECOME THE FINISHED COSTUMES.

When writing a full script, you will have to break down the story structure and be very meticulous in the way it plays out through the panels on every page. You can also decide the actual layout of the page, including how many panels to include and even their size. Conveying clear instructions from the writer to the artist is very important. If you describe an angry character in the script, make sure you add enough details so the artist will get that emotion across visually. State up front if the character's teeth are bared, his fists are clenched, or whether his eyes are narrowed or wide. Provide clear descriptions and instructions.

As you can see in the sample script page of Paladin Alpha (*right, and opposite page*), there are a number of cinematic-style directions, from medium views to close-ups and the individual visual elements in the panels that needed emphasis. The dialogue balloons are numbered for the convenience of the letterer. The artist Matt Roberts translated the script as well as the stage directions into a well-designed and dramatically composed page.

By choosing the full-script method, both the writer and artist are working within a well-defined structure. However, it's a more time-consuming process for the writer, and often the artist may find following the instructions restrictive. If you are both artist and writer, following this method may be overkill. You may find the next method easier.

In this technique, known in the 1960s as the Marvel Method, the writer provides the penciler with the basic plot either as a detailed synopsis or a general overview. This allows the artist to interpret the story in the way he thinks best, taking the responsibility of breaking it down into panels and pages. The writer comes in after the art is penciled and provides the dialogue.

When using the Marvel Method, the writer turns over the responsibility of pacing and story structure to the artist, which can be a heavy burden even if the artist enjoys having a great deal of control over the visual elements.

PAGE FOUR:

Panel 1: Med. close view of PA's left hand and the gauntlet.

ROGUE o/p(1): Long have I coveted your gauntlet...in much the same way, I imagine, as your -our- Terran ancestors coveted Arthur's Excalibur or Roland's Durandal.

Panel 2: ROGUE walks closer to PA.

ROGUE(2): But unlike those fabled objects of power, I believe your gauntlet to be technological in nature, not mystical.

(3): I theorize that its energies exist in a "time pocket", fueled by the beginning of the universe when it was a primal monobloc with no dimensions of space...

Panel 3: Med. view of ROGUE, really getting into his dissertation, eyes gleaming avariciously. Plenty of neg. space.

ROGUE(4):...It taps into the quantum stream, drawing on the incalculable energies that were released in the first few picoseconds following the "Big Bang"...

(5):..Channelling the matrix of protoparticles that swirled through the universe before the physical laws as we know them fully stabilized.

(6): What could a man of true vision not accomplish with such a device at his command?!

Panel 4: ROGUE stands just outside the energy screen, smirking down at PA inside, who is lifting his head, his teeth bared in a silent snarl.

ROGUE(7): At any rate, once your physical form is consigned to the quantum stream, you'll be beyond all caring. However, your gauntlet will remain behind. A memento of your visit.

(8): See you down the stream, "Alpha."

Panel 5: Inside the field of energy, PA is becoming transparent. His gauntlet remains solid, but it sprouts a dozen energy probes that strike the field and penetrate it. ROGUE reacts in fear as they zero in on him from a dozen different directions.

PA(9): Do you really think you're the first megalomaniac who has ever tried to steal a Paladin's gauntlet..?

(10):...And do you think there are no safeguards to prevent it?

Veteran Marvel artist Don Heck told interviewer Les Daniels that it took him a while to adjust to this practice: "Stan (Lee) would call me up and he'd give me the first couple of pages over the phone and the last page. I'd say, 'What about the stuff in between?' and he'd say, 'Fill it in.'"

While he was working on *The Whisperer in Darkness*, Heck was asked which method he preferred, the plot-first or the full-script method.

Paladin Alpha's script page (*left*) and finished page (*right*).

He responded, "Full script—don't make *me* do all the work!" However, some artists prefer the Marvel Method because it allows them to achieve their full potential, both as graphic storytellers and artists. Our preferred method is the thumbnail breakdown system. It works well for both scripter and artist. With this technique, the writer provides a rough sketch of each page, giving an idea of different perspectives ("camera" angles) and even indicating where the dialogue balloons are to be placed so as to achieve the best balance between the text and the visuals.

This method can be more time consuming for the writer than even full script, but in the long run it eases the responsibility on the artist because you have already storyboarded it, controlling the pacing and even indicating different lighting effects. You can see how artist Darryl Banks followed a crude layout to create a beautiful finished page (*below and opposite page*).

The Miskatonic Project © 2006 Mark Ellis, art by Don Heck.

▲ Artist Don Heck preferred the full-script method on *The Whisper in Darkness* graphic novel.

Darryl Banks's layout reference (*left*) and finished page (*right*).

From Concept to Layout

Most writers claim they can find stories anywhere, a dictum that the scriptwriters of the *Seinfeld* TV series proved on a weekly basis. The greatest source of fiction is life itself, even if that life is someone else's. The seeds of any kind of fiction, whether told in straight prose or the graphic narrative, are planted everywhere; therefore, you don't need to wait for inspiration before beginning to write. Often inspiration comes from engaging in the creative process itself, developing an idea into a vague concept and then into a solid premise on which to build a story.

One area of comics scripting that is no different from other forms of writing is developing your concept. Once you've settled on the basic idea for the graphic novel—the blueprint, so to speak—then you should start laying the foundation.

After thinking your concept through, place it within the context of your fictional world. It must seem real to the reader, even if it's an alien or fantasy world. Reader identification is essential, because without that readers will have difficulty suspending their sense of disbelief. In this stage you should strive to make your story as coherent, clear, and strong as possible. Visualize your concept by finding pictures that best suit your story's setting and characters. You can stimulate your imagination in this way by highlighting various scenes you want to see in the completed work.

However, since this is the graphic narrative form, all of your ideas and visualizations should be in service to the overarching story. Keep the concept in mind, but remember it must be adapted into a graphic dramatization. A good rule of thumb is to reserve pages with the fewest panels for action sequences. If you're working with an artist, always be conscious of how you describe action, setting, and background. Think like an artist and try to translate your concept and ideas visually.

E-FACT

THE MAN WHO HAS WRITTEN THE MOST COMICS, ACCORDING TO *THE GUINNESS BOOK OF WORLD RECORDS*, IS PAUL S. NEWMAN (NO RELATION TO THE ACTOR). HE IS CREDITED WITH SCRIPTING OVER 4,000 STORIES WRITTEN FOR 360 INDIVIDUAL TITLES, RESULTING IN MORE THAN 32,000 PAGES OF COMICS. DURING THE 1950S, HE WROTE BETWEEN 1,000 AND 2,000 PAGES PER YEAR.

A good way to shorten the distance between the writer and artist is to meet one another halfway. Lay out the graphic novel as a storyboard, sketching what you think needs to be conveyed on every page. The storyboard layouts can be as complete or as loose as you prefer, from fairly finished sketches to stick figures.

This approach is common among screenwriters and animators. Even novelists employ the storyboard technique. It permits the artist/writer team to examine the plot points from different perspectives, find weak areas in the script, and make the necessary changes.

THE LATE MICKEY SPILLANE STARTED HIS WRITING CAREER SCRIPTING FOR TIMELY COMICS, THE FIRST INCARNATION OF THE COMPANY THAT WOULD EVENTUALLY BECOME MARVEL. IN THE LATE 1940S, HE CREATED A PRIVATE-EYE CHARACTER FOR COMIC BOOKS, BUT BECAUSE OF THE SATURATION IN THE MARKETPLACE, HE TURNED THE CONCEPT INTO A NOVEL AND THUS WAS BORN *I, THE JURY*, THE FIRST IN THE BEST-SELLING MIKE HAMMER SERIES.

With this method you can pinpoint where the story's big moments should occur, even rearrange them for maximum dramatic effect. You can shift your main characters and main scenes. You can decide whether they need to be expanded or reduced. Don't fear altering your concept in order to put it in the best possible shape, and don't hesitate to jettison characters and ideas that you are struggling with.

Dialogue Says It All

Writing real-sounding (as opposed to realistic) dialogue is probably the most essential skill you should develop before scripting your graphic novel. In the comics form, many scenes, from big to small, rely almost exclusively on dialogue to solidify character and carry the plot forward. Although dialogue does not take the place of other important storytelling elements, you will depend on it much more than if you were writing a straight prose narrative.

Listen to how people talk, paying close attention to rhythm and vocabulary. Apply that to the voices of your characters. Hear them speak in your imagination, and listen for the qualities that distinguish them from one another. Reading written dialogue aloud often helps the process. However, there is a major difference between real-sounding and realistic dialogue. In the latter, people often stammer, digress, use "uh," or pepper conversation with slang and profanity. Real-sounding dialogue is not what you would hear actual people on the street say; it's a contrivance, a writer's approximation that has been streamlined and edited down for dramatic effect. The dialogue in movies is often as to the point as that in comics scripts.

E-SSENTIAL

FAMED ITALIAN MOVIE DIRECTOR FEDERICO FELLINI WAS A LIFELONG FAN OF COMICS. HIS SOLO DIRECTING DEBUT WAS A COMEDY CALLED *THE WHITE SHEIK*, ABOUT A HONEYMOONING COUPLE WHO BECOME SEPARATED ON THEIR TRIP TO ROME. THE HUSBAND BECOMES ENTANGLED WITH PROSTITUTES AND THE WIFE ENTERS THE WORLD OF HER FAVORITE COMIC BOOK HERO, THE WHITE SHEIK.

In prose, the practice of writing dialogue in a dialect is frowned upon, but it has been an accepted convention in the comics form for many decades. For example, if one of your characters is a 1930s gangster from Brooklyn, he might speak in the vernacular of the time, such as "youse" and "dese" for "you" and "these."

In the graphic narrative, learning to balance the dialogue with the action is an important consideration. The pacing of a page, the rhythm of the action in the panels, must be taken into account so the dialogue accommodates it, not impedes it. Will Eisner pointed out that there is an almost mathematical relationship between the placement of word balloons and the composition of the individual panels in which they appear.

The writer and the artist should strive to suggest the illusion of a brief time lapse in a dialogue exchange between characters. In a sequence from *Lakota* (*below*), artist Jim Mooney struck the perfect balance between the dialogue balloons and the composition. He altered the perspectives and matched the facial expressions to the information being conveyed. In this way, character was established and the plot advanced in a seamless blending of words and art.

Lakota.

Death Hawk © 2006 Mark Ellis, art by Rik Levins.

Unfortunately, one of the perennial drawbacks of relying on dialogue to move the plot and solidify character is that the artist may find himself illustrating a series of static talking-head panels. This is an all-too-common pitfall, but the writer and artist can work around it while developing the storyboard. Scenes should be written that serve as visual counterpoints and complements to the dialogue without overwhelming the art.

⬙ The imaginative layout of this page relies mainly on the visuals to establish the situation and setting, while the dialogue between the disguised Death Hawk and the corrupt Governor Quintus provides the reader with more of the back story.

TEAM BUILDING

Most graphic novels are produced by a team, with each phase of production being the responsibility of a different person. Even if you're working alone, eventually you will reach a point where you'll have to divvy up the labor among the different members of the production team. As this book is written for both those who are planning to produce a graphic novel as a single vision and for those who are fortunate enough to have the resources of a team, this chapter covers what is required for the completion of your project regardless of your situation.

Different Hats

If you look at each component of the graphic novel as a construction project, with each member of the crew assigned to a special skill area, then you'll be able to work methodically toward building a final, complete structure. But remember when you work with a team, you'll have to coordinate your efforts and be respectful of each other's strengths and expertise. If the writer and penciler collaborate closely, all other aspects of the project will fall into place much more harmoniously.

E-FACT

JACK KIRBY IS POPULARLY ACKNOWLEDGED BY COMICS CREATORS AND FANS AS ONE OF THE MOST INFLUENTIAL ARTISTS IN THE HISTORY OF COMICS. HIS OUTPUT WAS LEGENDARY, WITH ONE COUNT ESTIMATING THAT HE PRODUCED OVER **25,000** PAGES DURING HIS LIFETIME. IN **2006** HE WAS VOTED THE NUMBER-ONE ARTIST ON *COMIC BOOK RESOURCES'* ALL-TIME TOP *100* WRITERS AND ARTISTS.

Naturally, if the scripter and penciler are the same person, it isn't hard to coordinate things to ensure everyone is on the same page, but that arrangement may present its own unique and different problems at some later stage, mainly those derived from not having the many benefits of collaboration.

The old cliché about two heads being better than one does have its merits, not the least of which is having someone to watch your back, double-check your spelling and research, and generate ideas that you hadn't thought of, not to mention halving your workload.

The Writer

The story itself begins in the imagination of the writer. Regardless of the arguments and discussions over the years about whether the writer or the artist is the most important contributor, the process can't even begin without the basic idea or concept, the infrastructure upon which the graphic elements are based.

To write a graphic narrative you'll need the same skill set as any other writer—a facility with language, knowledge of grammar and the rules of punctuation, and a good imagination. You'll also need to understand the fundamentals of storytelling, and that begins with the framework.

The framework is the underlying theme that serves as the focal point of the narrative. The creators must give the reader a framework that is immediately and easily recognizable. This is one reason that superheroes have been such a mainstay in comics for so many decades. Yet commercial considerations sometimes limit the thematic range of the graphic novel.

Star Rangers © 2006 Mark Ellis.

◀ Artist Jim Mooney developed an innovative method of minimizing monotonous talking-head scenes.

The theme does not have to be complicated or even particularly original to grab the reader, but you must be sure it is a theme your artist feels strongly about. When putting the framework together, keep in mind the importance of character development. Be conscious of striking a balance between all of the following elements: theme, plot, setting, storytelling, and characterization.

Always strive to build reader identification and empathy for your characters. Although the theme isn't necessarily the major component of the finished work, the form itself is very important. The comics storyteller must think in visual terms, building the story through a series of images utilizing a type of visual shorthand similar to a screenplay.

The writer's eye and the artist's eye are equally important when working in the graphic narrative form. If, as the writer, you are going to let your imagination run wild, you also need to be aware of the strengths and weaknesses of the artist and tailor your ideas to showcase his strengths.

For example, if you were working with an artist who is not experienced in drawing horses, you wouldn't want to write extensive scenes of cavalry charges. Write to your artist's strengths, not against them.

One of the axioms of fiction writing is "show, don't tell," and nowhere is this more appropriate than in the graphic narrative. Reduce the number of static talking-head scenes and avoid them altogether whenever possible.

However, in instances where the narrative must be the dominant feature of a page or a sequence, you have little choice other than to let the text do the job of carrying the story forward. In this case, particular care needs to be paid to keep the writing strong and focused.

The Artists

Whether a graphic novel is successful is often due to the penciler. If and when you wear the artist's hat, you'll find out very quickly the nature of the graphic narrative requires you to do more than just draw pretty pictures or do character sketches. The artist creates the whole world in which the story takes place. You only have seconds to get the reader's attention. In a novel or short story, the opening line or narrative hook is consciously designed to grab the interest of the reader. In a graphic novel, the artist must rely on the first visual—often a splash page—to keep the reader turning pages.

This is often achieved by presenting a powerful and memorable image combined with evocative text. More attention and care is frequently lavished on this page of a comic book or graphic novel than on any other.

▶ In an adaptation of Sir Arthur Conan Doyle's *Lot No. 249*, artist Darryl Banks established the atmosphere of the story in this beautifully detailed opening splash page.

Just as the writer must know grammar, punctuation, and sentence structure, the comic artist must understand character design, perspective, proportion, light and dark values, and, perhaps most importantly, how to tell a story in a sequence of images. Although the artist has a bit more freedom than the writer to utilize caricatures rather than ultrarealistic renderings of people and places, the context must still be accepted as believable by the reader. To endow her images with atmosphere the artist may choose to use solid black masses or render the backgrounds in a minimalistic sketchy style. The range is infinite.

The penciler lays out the fictional world, the inker follows his lines, hopefully interpreting them faithfully, then the colorist brings the black and white world to life and sets the mood with her own interpretation of the original art. The letterer is an artist, too, and you'll learn more about her role in the next section of this chapter.

One of the main reasons superheroes have been essential in comics for so many decades is that, until recently, they were very difficult to believably present in other media, such as film.

The comics artists who drew them were unrestricted by the confines of realism. Jack Kirby, the undisputed King of Comics, was legendary for his powerful drawings and grand imagination, which often outstripped the ideas of his many writer-collaborators.

E-FACT

WHAT DO WIDOWS, FIREFLIES, AND BURSTS HAVE IN COMMON? THESE ARE ALL TERMS USED TO TALK ABOUT TYPOGRAPHY OR EFFECTS USED IN THE COMICS LETTERING PROCESS. WIDOWS ARE LINES OF TEXT THAT STAND ALONE, AND FIREFLIES ARE THE THREE SHORT LINES PLACED BEFORE AND AFTER SIGHS AND GASPS. BURSTS ARE JAGGED-EDGE BALLOONS THAT CONTAIN SOUND EFFECTS OR SHOUTED DIALOGUE.

When working with a writer, all the artists involved in the project must translate the scripter's descriptions and words into images, but they need not mindlessly follow the letter of the script. As in the case of Jack Kirby, individual style and approach frequently enhances the script, not hinders it. Be sure to discuss your ideas with the scripter when possible, as a radical departure from the script could conceivably cause future problems.

Certain kinds of stories are best illustrated with certain types of styles, appropriate to the theme and content. However, the skills of many artists are quite versatile, even if they prefer one genre over another.

For example, Don Heck was known for his many years of work on Marvel superhero titles, yet he felt his best work was featured in less flamboyant stories, such as the characters of *The Miskatonic Project*. The artist should focus on the kind of narrative that best suits his style, if for nothing else, so that he and the writer will share the same voice and vision.

Although artist Don Heck was best known for his work on Marvel superheroes, he preferred drawing noncostumed characters such as *The Miskatonic Project*.

Art by Don Heck, *The Miskatonic Project* © 2006 Mark Ellis.

▲ Sound effects, such as this in a panel from *The Miskatonic Project*, punch up the action in the scene.

The Letterer

What many people do not realize (until they try to do it themselves) is that lettering is really an artform. The work of the letterer not only conveys the spoken word in the form of narrative and dialogue, but it also depicts sound effects that enhance the reader's perception of what is taking place on the page. Poorly done lettering and sound effects can detract and distract, so great attention to detail is essential here.

The letterer is not only responsible for word balloons but also bursts, sound effects, and titles. She is usually a person who is very familiar with comics, highly skilled in lettering, and has some general knowledge of typography.

▶ Tightly lettered and legible word balloons are integral to the overall look of a comics page.

For more on lettering, recommended resources are the *DC Comics Guide to Coloring and Lettering Comics* and the Online Gallery of Dale Marting: A Foolproof Method of Comic Book Hand Lettering (***http://home.swbell.net/grizmart/lettering.html***).

Hand lettering requires great skill, patience, and practice, practice, practice. Hand letterers are worthy of great respect and appreciation for their skills, not only in calligraphy but also in the artistic depiction and placement of word balloons and sound effects. Although traditionally letterers have worked directly on the original artwork, they only did so after they had thoroughly learned their art. Develop your lettering skills on practice paper and save the original artwork until you feel very confident that you can do a professional job.

Colorists

Color plays an important role by focusing attention on important points of the narrative. It sets mood and conveys atmosphere quite effectively, too. While coloring may not be within your budget (if you are self publishing), it's still good to have some general knowledge on this topic.

As penciling and inking is an art, so is the work of the colorist, although in years past it was the work of craftsmen. Before the advent of computers, color printing used the cut-color process for separating colors into CMYK (cyan, magenta, yellow, and black). The process used by comic book companies was to color photostats of their black line drawings and use acetate overlays to represent the different CMYK colors, which were then made into negatives and burned onto printing plates for the four-color process.

Three pieces of acetate were lined up on top of each other over the artwork page. Where the film was cut away from the acetate, ink would not print. Where the film remained, the camera negative would leave a blank spot and ink would print.

If this sounds complex, that's because it is. It also explains why early comic books printed on newsprint used a limited color palette, almost always solid greens, reds, blues, and yellows. The color sections of the Sunday comic strips had a wider range of colors available to them.

E-FACT

CHARLTON COMICS, A PUBLISHING COMPANY BASED IN DERBY, CONNECTICUT, THAT EXISTED FROM 1946 TO 1986, WAS INFAMOUS FOR HAVING THE WORST COLORING IN THE COMICS FIELD. THEIR OLD PRINTING PRESS HAD BEEN BUILT PRIMARILY TO PRINT THE COLORS ON CEREAL BOXES, AND THE IMAGES ON THEIR COMIC BOOK COVERS WERE OFTEN BLURRED AND INDISTINCT.

Dr. Martin's Dyes were the industry standard for coloring comics for decades. These watercolor inks enabled the colorist to achieve a nuanced and sophisticated effect never achievable by cut color. Most color processing in the first fifty years of comic book production was rushed if not downright crude. However, in the late 1980s and early 1990s, colorists began using Adobe Photoshop and other software. Now almost all comics and graphic novels are colored on computers, and a vast palette of hues, gradients, and effects are now available.

CHAPTER 7

THE STORY BECOMES ART

How does one get from the story and plot to the sequence of images that make up a finished graphic novel? This chapter describes the collaboration and cooperation required between the principals involved. Ideally the scripter, penciler, inker, letterer, and colorist will all be on the same page, pun intended.

Layout and Design

The style of art establishes the tone of the novel, but design and layouts are equally important in the success of a graphic novel. This is a major difference between mass-produced comic books and graphic novels.

Although many comics artists are natural designers (Alex Toth, Will Eisner, and Darryl Banks come to mind), not everyone's design skills are that good. If in doubt about technical issues, it's a good idea to consult with someone who has a background in publication layout and design. A very helpful resource in this area is *Panel Discussions: Design in Sequential Art Storytelling*, by Durwin Talon, Will Eisner, Walter Simonson, Mike Mignola, and Mark Schultz.

Early comic books were composed and laid out for children who were just learning to read. The panel sequence was very straightforward with four rows of two panels each for a total of eight panels per page. Only rarely did this structure vary. Fortunately for readers, the rigidity of page and panel layout was loosened considerably starting in the 1960s.

▶ In this beautifully designed and laid out page from *Lot No. 249*, artist Darryl Banks establishes characterization and moves the story forward without the traditional panel grid.

Lot No. 249 © 2006 Mark Ellis.

To envision how your completed novel will look, create a prototype, or *dummy*, by folding 8½ x 11-inch sheets of paper in half and arranging them so they will have the same page count as you want for your novel. The first page of the story will usually fall onto a right-hand page. Don't forget to factor in pages for the title, copyright, and other information pages. Begin laying out your story using thumbnail sketches of the action with the goal in mind of planning the overall guide you will follow.

E-FACT

DURING COMICS' GOLDEN AGE, ONE NOTABLE EXCEPTION TO THE EIGHT-PANELS-PER-PAGE RULE WAS MAX GAINES OF EC COMICS, WHO IN THE EARLY 1950s ENCOURAGED HIS STABLE OF ARTISTS TO DEVELOP IDIOSYNCRATIC STYLES, INCLUDING EXPERIMENTAL PAGE AND PANEL LAYOUTS. UNLIKE THE STANDARD OF PUBLISHERS AT THE TIME, WHICH MAINTAINED ARTIST ANONYMITY, EC PUBLISHED ONE-PAGE BIOGRAPHIES OF ALL THEIR ARTISTS IN THEIR COMIC BOOKS.

Also keep in mind that experimenting with panel size on the page can affect the pacing of the story, either speeding it up or slowing it down. Although many artists are quite experimental with their layouts, sometimes the storytelling suffers because it becomes difficult for the reader to understand panel flow. It's best to keep the layout easy to follow.

Character Design

There are a number of standard design types that can be used for character reference. Years ago it was an accepted practice to stick strictly to stereotypes—mad scientists were bald and wore white coats, good girls were blond, bad girls brunette, and so forth. Although elements of these stereotypical models are still in use, they aren't quite as limited as in previous decades.

The basic design of your cast of characters should engage the reader's attention without too much introductory explanation. Obviously, a page featuring a beautiful woman and handsome man will be perceived favorably—this reaction seems to be hard-wired into human nature. However, if that beautiful woman and handsome man are vampires, then the design will have to be by necessity a bit unusual. Fangs, eye shape, even clothing styles will have to be considered.

E-FACT

WILL EISNER SUGGESTED USING ANIMAL-BASED IMAGES AS THE TEMPLATE FOR CHARACTER DESIGN, BELIEVING THAT USING FACIAL OR BODY TYPES SUGGESTIVE OF LIONS OR SNAKES ESTABLISHED PERSONALITY TYPES UPON THE READER'S FIRST GLANCE, SINCE FACIAL CONFIGURATIONS AND POSTURES ESTABLISHED WHETHER THE CHARACTER WAS FRIENDLY OR DANGEROUS.

▲ In *Death Hawk: The Soulworm Saga*, beautiful women and handsome men are not necessarily good people.
▼ Superheroes are traditionally presented larger than life, taller and broader than ordinary people.

If your graphic novel features fairly realistic characters, the artist will need to be very aware of the importance of proportion and body type. These can be affected by different drawing styles for different genres. For example, in a novel about super-powered characters, the cast would be rendered with exaggerated musculature and height. The rule of thumb is that superheroes are always drawn a head taller than nonpowered characters.

If your art is more cartoonlike in nature, then you will have more freedom to play with physiques and facial types. Comic strip style characters usually have large heads atop disproportionately small, childlike bodies. A character with big eyes is usually gullible or innocent, and a character with narrowed eyes represents strength, intelligence, and a resolute nature.

Clothing styles are a tried and true method of employing visual shorthand to establish a character type. A woman in a slinky dress is instantly identified as a femme fatale without a word of text describing her as such. However, a mysterious man wearing a trench coat, dark glasses, and carrying a gun could be a criminal, a detective, or a secret agent. It's not clear whether he's a good guy or a bad guy at first glance.

There is a common set of character types that populate every graphic novel or comic book. They have been used over and over again with only slight variations since the form began, and the artist should use these types as templates for his own creations.

Art by Jim Mooney, *Colonel Wildfire* © 2006 Mark Ellis.

◀ Many artists have their own set of character types they rely on.

Preparing a model sheet of the main cast of characters to serve as a reference guide should be done early in the project. Artist Jim Mooney drew the primary cast of the Star Rangers (*below*) so he could tell at a glance their heights, weights, and proportions relative to one another. It is a tremendously useful tool for everyone involved with the project, from writer to colorist.

Star Rangers © 2006 Mark Ellis.

Art by Don Heck, *The Miskatonic Project* © 2006 Mark Ellis.

▲ Lord Sabbath of the Miskatonic Project is a mysterious figure who typifies the concept of the morally ambiguous character.

◀ Artist Jim Mooney prepared a model sheet of the original Star Rangers cast before he began work on the title.

Panel Design

Finding a way to completely immerse the reader in a story is the purview of both the scripter and artists, but often the lion's share of the design work, particularly panel design, falls upon the penciler. It is here that you must call on all your storytelling expertise to present the tale in such a way as to first grab attention and then hold it.

The seamless flow of image from panel to panel and page to page does not always come easily. Beginners are helped by creating the aforementioned dummy and laying out the scenes in thumbnail form first. By this time you should have a sense of the story, its tone and its mood. With a character sheet and script in hand, further plan your panel layout and page design. Read through the script to be sure you thoroughly understand it—if you don't, how can the reader? Then give your imagination free rein. To move the plot along, most pages have four to six panels. Pages with complicated images require bigger panels, so fewer panels should be drawn on the page. You should also be conscious of the story momentum when you make the decision about the number of panels per page or their size. Lots of small panels tend to slow down the flow.

Jim Mooney's splash/title page for *A Trip to Necropolis* is moody and atmospheric, and all the elements from art to text work together.

Next you will begin to jot down and draw key plot points. As you sketch these out from the movie in your head (perhaps with the aid of thumbnails from the writer), you will be able to better gauge the pacing necessary for the scenes you are depicting. If the writer has provided roughs or thumbnails, all the better, but remember, they are there to help you, not to be slavishly followed!

Likewise, you can use other comics work for inspiration, but make sure the design is uniquely your own, not a weak reflection of some other artist's work. If you've been paying close attention to design, you'll have noticed the impact individual panel design and even gutter size (the space between panels) can have on the story. Be imaginative and make use of layout, lighting, camera angle, and pacing to tell the tale dramatically. *Wizard: How To Draw*, from Wizard Entertainment, has basic training tutorials as well as a section on panel design, lettering, and coloring.

Splash Pages

In comics vocabulary, a splash page is simply a full page of art. Often used on the first page to draw the reader in, the splash usually contains the title and credits. It also serves to establish the setting, time, and even the primary characters of the story.

Splash pages that aren't on the first page are called interior splashes. These pages may include titles and credits; that is your call. An interior panel that is bigger than the others is called a splash panel. Splashes shouldn't be overused. If there isn't a good reason to have them, such as a plot point that must be made or a fantastic visual waiting to be portrayed, just skip them. They should always be reserved for dramatic or momentous visuals.

Because larger panels serve to break up the monotony of pages divided into multi-panel spreads, they have great visual impact and usually portray a moment of importance and drama in the story. Done well, they vary the predictable rhythm of the page and help hold the reader's interest.

E-FACT

SPLASH PAGES ARE USED LESS THESE DAYS IN REGULAR COMICS BECAUSE SPACE IS AT A PREMIUM WHEN YOU HAVE TWENTY-TWO PAGES TO TELL A STORY. HOWEVER, THEY ARE APPROPRIATE AND NOT AN INDULGENCE WHEN USED IN GRAPHIC NOVELS WHERE THANKS TO THE HIGHER PAGE COUNT YOU HAVE THE LUXURY OF TELLING MORE OF THE STORY.

Double-Page Spread

Interior splashes may cross over the central gutter to the facing page, in which case they are called double splashes or a double-page spread.

▶ This double-page spread from *Lakota* features the main characters and a dramatic turning point in the plot.

Art by Jim Mooney, Lakota © 2006 Mark Ellis.

Double splashes should only be used when a point is reached in the story that demands a *really* strong visual, a scene of epic proportions that is integral to the plot.

Since your job is to make the most effective use of the space you have, the double splash must be an image that conveys vital information in a way that only it possibly could. It is a necessity-driven image. If the image could fit into a smaller panel and have the same impact, then don't bother blowing it up to double-page spread size. Ineffective and unnecessary double splashes are embarrassing; it looks as if you're trying to pad out the story.

In an innovative move, artist Jim Steranko designed two double-page spreads into his Nick Fury, Agent of S.H.I.E.L.D., story in *Strange Tales* #167 (April 1969). If readers wanted to see how both the double-page spreads were intended to look, they had to buy two copies of that issue and lay them out side by side.

When splash pages are well done and necessary, they are a good thing because they draw the reader back to your book over and over again. What constitutes a good double-page spread? That depends on the script. The writer should have given a clear indication of what was considered the moment of high drama or impact in the story. That moment must be the right one for both scripter and artist.

CHAPTER 8

WRITER'S REQUIREMENTS

The fact that writers write and critics criticize is a truism, and it's especially true of a writer's inner critic. But the main requirement of writers is simply to write. It's actually easier to be inspired while writing than when you're not writing. But even if you have the inspiration and the overwhelming desire to write, you'll need the proper tools to bring your story to life, just like a sculptor needs a hammer and chisel and a painter her brush and palette. This chapter covers all these parts of your role as a graphic novelist.

Word Processors and Computers

It is hard to believe that not that long ago most preprint production and word processing in the comics field was done either by hand, in the case of the art, or on a typewriter or word processor, in the case of the script. Scriptwriters in the twenty-first century are indeed fortunate to have such tools as superfast computers and sophisticated software at their disposal.

Art by Rik Levins, *Death Hawk* © 2006 Mark Ellis.

▲ Computers have been a boon to writers and artists alike over the last twenty years.

It is mind-boggling how much time and energy can be saved by their use. Whether you're a Macintosh or PC user, an artist or a writer, a good computer setup isn't strictly speaking absolutely essential to the production of your graphic novel, but it surely will make your life a lot easier.

For years writers have been using Microsoft Word to compose their scripts. Although any word processing program will probably be sufficient to do the job, Word has universal appeal. Whatever software you choose, the ability to revise and edit work is a huge advantage to comics writers, who frequently have to deal with tricky pacing and strict page-count constraints.

Fortunately, writers don't require as much computing power as artists do, as their text files do not require a lot of computer memory, sophisticated graphics programs, or expensive flat-screen monitors. Plunk writers down in front of a low-end computer with little memory but with Internet access and a word processing program and they are in business.

These days computers are affordable and within the reach of most people. If money is tight, used and reconditioned models can be purchased for only a few hundred dollars. Sometimes manufacturers offer student discounts on new ones, and a quick search of the Web for major computer manufacturers will often turn up very sizeable discounts.

Research and Verisimilitude

You read about research earlier, but the depth of research actually boils down to the individual writer—how much you need to know about your topic depends on how in-depth you want your story to be.

Art by Robert Lewis, image © 2006 Mark Ellis.

△ Historical periods are favorites among writers and artists, even though they may not be strictly factual representations.

▷ Hal Foster's work on *Prince Valiant* was rightly admired for its attention to detail, although he often mixed different cultures and centuries for artistic effect.

As you write you'll learn to gauge how much raw material you'll actually need to build a believable storyline. Even if you're writing a story based on true incidents, there's always a mixture of fact and pure invention involved in the process. Even if you're dealing with a purely imagined setting, making it look, seem, and feel real is the job of both the writer and the artist. The artist can take reference material and either render it exactly or let his imagination (and skills) elaborate, revise, and exaggerate it.

The great Harold Foster, for example, during his decades-long tenure on the *Prince Valiant* newspaper strip, set a high standard for historical research accuracy and maintained authentic medieval detail even though the strip was actually set several hundred years before the medieval period.

Art by Hal Foster, © 2007 King Features Syndicate.

Sometimes an artist or writer's fixation on research becomes an inside joke. Chet Gould, the creator of *Dick Tracy*, was devoted to presenting police rules and procedures in such painstaking detail that it often interfered with the story. After an editorial comment that the strip was becoming a textbook, Gould reserved those tidbits for Crime Stoppers, small true-crime vignettes that were inserted near the title of the Sunday page. Due to the Crime Stoppers inserts, Gould received a number of awards and commendations from law enforcement agencies.

But even alien places can be presented in a believable fashion. In *Death Hawk: The Soulworm Saga*, Mark Ellis (coauthor of this book) wrote a pivotal sequence in a futuristic casino populated by various extraterrestrial races.

▶ In *Death Hawk: The Soulworm Saga*, a new game of chance was invented to make the twenty-fifth-century casino seem real.

Art by Adam Hughes, *Death Hawk* © 2006 Mark Ellis.

He also invented the game of Orbit that the characters play, describing the rules and even a play table. Artist Adam Hughes interpreted the script beautifully, adding his own touches with various background characters drawn from other science fiction properties, like a Martian Thark and even a Yoda look-alike wearing sunglasses. The result was a scene that had the feel of verisimilitude about it. You could almost smell the smoke and hear the murmur of alien voices and the clink of glasses.

Try to avoid the generic comic book setting, such as a standard city street or a government testing lab that has the stereotypical test tubes and giant computers. If you don't believe in your story, it's unlikely your readers will either.

▼ Hal Foster's *Prince Valiant* did not use word or dialogue balloons to tell the story but relied on descriptive text as in traditional illustrated novels.

Dialogue Balloons Versus Captions

Although most graphic narratives tell the story through a combination of images and dialogue balloons, some practitioners have relied mainly on captions, which was the preferred form of newspaper strips in the 1920s. Captions are blocks of descriptive text contained within square or rectangular boxes that either give the reader an insight into a character's thoughts and motivations or describe the image itself in greater detail. Captions are most useful when a writer prefers not to employ thought balloons to share a character's inner voice with the reader. However, when the text of a graphic novel is presented almost exclusively through captions, the end result is more of an illustrated novel. Harold Foster adopted the form of traditional book illustration for *Prince Valiant*.

Art by Hal Foster. © 2007 King Features Syndicate.

I FACE R'YEX FOR THE BETTER PART OF FIVE HOURS.

THE ATMOSPHERE GROWS HUMID WITH THE BITTER STINK OF GREED...AND AFTER A WHILE... *DESPERATION*.

CYKE INFORMS ME WHENEVER R'YEX ACTIVATES HIS INTER-FACE. I DON'T BOTHER TO OUTCHEAT HIM.

"ORBIT" FOR THE TENTH TIME STRAIGHT.

ALL I DO IS *BLEED* HIM.

ONCE MORE, DAMN YOU! EVERYTHING OR *NOTHING!!*

YOUR STAKE?

ON AMICUS, FEMALES ARE PROPERTY. R'YEX CAN DO WHAT HE WANTS WITH HER.

ACCEPTED.

HER AGAINST YOUR WINNINGS!

HEY! YOU CAN'T—!

AND HE'S FALLEN NEATLY INTO MY TRAP.

Art by Adam Hughes, *Death Hawk* © 2006 Mark Ellis.

This page from *Death Hawk: The Soulworm Saga* shows the balanced use of captions and dialogue balloons.

Because of this practice and others, Foster is considered more of an illustrator than a cartoonist—although he did win a number of cartooning awards. *Prince Valiant*, with its underreliance on text, remains a classic study of sequential illustration that depends primarily on the artwork to tell the story.

Used in tandem, dialogue balloons and captions can be balanced to permit greater reader identification, but a rhythm must be established. The breaking down of the story into panels and text is a matter of technique and style. Both Milton Caniff and Will Eisner were masters of the technique of combining the text and the visuals so that both equally carried the story. In their work, both men used text as a counterpoint to extreme visual action or employed visual metaphors to break up long sequences of dialogue.

If the text takes precedence over the images, then your work will be more of an illustrated rather than graphic novel. Separating the text from the art will make for a more leisurely paced narrative, since the reader is encouraged to spend more time and attention on the artwork alone.

Foster's draftsmanship and artwork was meticulously detailed; therefore, he did not want the individual panels cluttered with dialogue or thought balloons. Most of the time he enclosed his narrative text within the frame of the image.

As a general rule, dialogue balloons should contain a bare minimum of words, no more than twenty-five to thirty. Boxed captions contain more, but the writer should be very conscious of narrative redundancy. In other words, don't use a caption to describe what the characters have just said in a dialogue balloon or have it describe the actions of a panel, as in the example. In the early days of the graphic narrative, this kind of redundancy was a common failing among writers and artists who were not accustomed to working in the form.

For a brief instant the Corporal and Ling faced each other like gladiators of old . . . Slowly the Chinese drew a knife . . . "The Corporal!" he whispered. "Delivered into my hands!" . . . A grim smile spread over the Mountie's face . . .

▲ Avoid describing in a caption something that is obvious in the art, as in this example from the early days of comic books. Public domain image.

E-FACT

THE RUBEN AWARD IS GIVEN ANNUALLY BY THE NATIONAL CARTOONISTS SOCIETY AND IS NAMED IN HONOR OF RUBE GOLDBERG. THE AWARD IS GIVEN TO ARTISTS WHO ARE VOTED THE CARTOONIST OF THE YEAR BY SOCIETY MEMBERS. IN 1985, FOR BETTER OR FOR WORSE CARTOONIST LYNN JOHNSTON WAS THE FIRST FEMALE CARTOONIST TO WIN THIS AWARD. IN THE LATE 1990S THE NATIONAL CARTOONISTS SOCIETY ANNOUNCED THAT NO CARTOONIST CAN WIN THE AWARD MORE THAN ONCE.

Sometimes dialogue balloons can impede the narrative flow and jar the reader out of her suspension of disbelief. Care must be taken so that the balloons or captions do not become the dominant feature of a panel.

Visual Thinking and Pacing

There is an old saying among comic scripters and screenwriters: To write visually you have to think visually. An easy exercise to help with the visualization of a story is to pay attention to various dramatic or comedic cues on your favorite TV series or movie.

Watch for the kind of emotion that actors project when they are angry or frightened, and pay attention to how they convey these emotions without a word of dialogue being spoken. The angle of the eyebrows, the set of the mouth, facial lines—all these cues will help you know the thoughts of the characters.

Lakota © 2006 Mark Ellis.

▲ Artist Don Heck used a minimum of pencil lines to convey extreme emotions such as anger.

Visualization

If you're writing a graphic novel set on the windswept plains of Mars, then you would most effectively convey the sense of barrenness primarily through images. You wouldn't have characters sitting around in a room talking about how barren and cold Mars is when a single visual would convey that better.

Visualize the page and figure out if there are too few or too many panels to keep the story moving. If there is little physical action on the page but lots of expository dialogue instead, minimize the number of panels so it won't seem like frame after frame of talking heads. Even during a scene that is more talk than action, the storyteller must be sure to employ gestures and postures easily recognizable with the tone of the dialogue, whether it is meant to convey anger, sadness, or humor.

E-FACT

HENRY, A LONG-RUNNING NEWSPAPER COMIC STRIP, ACTUALLY BEGAN WITH DIALOGUE, BUT LATER THE CREATOR, CARL ANDERSON, DECIDED TO HAVE THE CHARACTERS EXPRESS THEMSELVES STRICTLY IN PANTOMIME. BECAUSE IT WAS ESSENTIALLY A SILENT STRIP, IT WAS VERY POPULAR ABROAD BECAUSE THERE WAS NO TEXT TO TRANSLATE.

On the other hand, if there is a great deal of physical action, you don't want to overuse captions and dialogue balloons, which will interfere with the flow. Remember, a page should flow artistically and dramatically. A graphic narrative exists to tell a story.

The Miskatonic Project © 2006 Mark Ellis.

◀ In this page from *Lakota*, Jim Mooney's choice of facial expressions and postures conveys the tension between the two characters.

Pacing Your Novel

When you establish the pace of your novel, in reality you're setting the pace of each page. Some writers insist on ending each page with some sort of little kicker, or even a big kicker, a trick or device that makes the reader inclined to read on whether it's the end of a scene or not. I personally prefer to end a scene on the last panel of a page to make the scene self-contained. I continue a new scene on the following page.

Although comics scripting has its own techniques with rules that must be followed, the act of writing itself is not a hard and fast science. Writers should experiment, striving for a style or method that feels best for them. The more you write and the more you experiment, the more you will learn, and eventually you'll find the style that best suits you. Ideally, the pace of your graphic novel should always move the story forward both in plot and character.

PENCILER'S REQUIREMENTS

Now it's time to get into the nitty gritty. This chapter explains the tools, skills, circumstances, and space necessary to maintain a productive atmosphere and workflow in the penciler's environment. This space has distinct needs from that of the scripter, inker, colorist, and letterer. This chapter provides a breakdown of the steps necessary to setting up a workspace and a checklist of the minimum tools necessary to get started on your graphic novel.

Workspace and Tools

The penciler on a comics or graphic novel project requires a work area large enough to contain a drafting table and a stand or shelf to hold art supplies and reference materials. This can be in a corner of your bedroom or in an expensive office suite, but wherever it is, it must be a space where you can concentrate and work on the project without interruption or having to put away your book and set it up again every time you want to work. A T-square, ruler, triangle, good lighting, Bristol board, and pencils are also among the bare necessities. A location with good natural light augmented by an artificial light source is the ideal setup. Obviously there is no substitute for natural light, but you'll want to be able to arrange your setup to work when natural daylight is unavailable.

E-FACT

GRAPHIC NOVELS ARE BECOMING INCREASINGLY POPULAR IN THE U.S. MARKET. NEIL GAIMAN'S SANDMAN SERIES, PUBLISHED UNDER THE VERTIGO IMPRINT BY DC COMICS, HAS SO FAR BEEN THE MOST SUCCESSFUL GRAPHIC NOVEL SERIES IN THE UNITED STATES. THE ORIGINAL COMIC BOOK SERIES WAS COLLECTED INTO BOOK FORM, WITH ESTIMATED SALES OF OVER ONE MILLION COPIES.

Although it is axiomatic that a penciler must use a pencil, which pencil should be your choice? There are many to choose from, but it always comes down to personal preference.

Your choice may range from wood to mechanical pencils, with leads of varying hardness. Some artists prefer light blue nonrepro pencils, such as Col-Erase brand erasable 1298 nonphoto blue pencil for roughs and Illustrator brand blue Mirage 1360 XX-Fine Point nonrepro blue marker for tight final pencils. You can even use Staedtler Mars Special 12 #0.5 nonphoto blue technical pencil leads if you can't find the Mirage 1360. The blue lines drawn with them tend to disappear or drop out when photographed by graphics cameras and scanners during the prepress process, and as a bonus you don't have to worry about erasing mistakes as the lines disappear in any case. Many pencilers choose to use the harder lead pencils for their rough initial work as they produce a rather light line, then finish with a softer lead that produces a darker line. It is a personal preference, and lots of experimentation will be the only way to discover what works best for you.

E-QUESTION
WHAT IS THE XERIC FOUNDATION?

THE XERIC FOUNDATION IS A PRIVATE, NONPROFIT CORPORATION ESTABLISHED BY PETER LAIRD, OF TEENAGE MUTANT NINJA TURTLES FAME. IT OFFERS FINANCIAL ASSISTANCE TO SELF-PUBLISHING COMIC BOOK CREATORS. TO QUALIFY THE ARTIST MUST LIVE IN THE UNITED STATES OR CANADA AND BE A CITIZEN AND CURRENT RESIDENT OF EITHER COUNTRY. SEE **www.xericfoundation.com/xericwhat.html** FOR MORE INFORMATION.

In the United States, the paper size frequently used is 11 × 17-inch Bristol board, in finishes from smooth to rough. This is reduced after the inking and lettering is complete to the finished page size of 6½ × 10¼ inches, which minimizes slight mistakes and makes the overall image look remarkably crisp and clean.

It is important to use good quality paper, such as the products in the Strathmore line. Strathmore is a very good quality art paper and is widely available. It may cost a bit more, but using professional quality products will help you produce professional results.

This paper also allows the artist to use charcoal and pastels as well as inks to finish the work if he is so inclined. This is important since the inker will be going over the penciled lines.

It is vital to master the drafting basics: straight lines, corners that meet, a clean page with few erasures and no smudges or fingerprints. This means the penciler will need the help of an erasing shield and a kneaded rubber eraser. The shield protects images adjacent to the area that need to be cleaned up from accidental erasure. It is the mark of an experienced artist to draw lines that are square.

Death Hawk © 2006 by Mark Ellis.

🔺 Subtle changes were made to Darryl Banks's pencils by inker Robert Lewis—note the difference in the linework on the woman's facial expression.

This means the vertical lines bisect the horizontal ones to form perfect 90 degree corners. You should practice creating borders that are truly straight and square by drawing horizontal lines with the T-square and vertical lines with the triangle resting on the T-square. A bit of practice on cheaper paper will save wasting the more expensive Bristol board. Remember, too, that the industry standard for a gutter is $3/16$".

Here are a few online sources for Bristol board:

- *https://westfieldcomics.com/wow/supply.html*
- *www.misterart.com/store/browse/001/cat_id/741/Art-Supplies-Paper--Boards-Paper-Bristol-Paper.htm*
- *www.dickblick.com/categories/artboards*

A note about reference material and swipe files: All pencilers develop an extensive library from which they draw inspiration and use for reference. This of course doesn't mean brazen tracing or copying. If you start out relying on the work of others for all your drawing, it won't truly be your own and your distinct style will never have an opportunity to grow and develop. Wise artists also practice drawing from life whenever the opportunity arises, as it produces a more fluid style and more realistic anatomy. Not that a lot of comic book anatomy is realistic, but you do have to know the rules before you can break them.

Developing a Graphic Storytelling Style

Chances are if you are a comics fan you have a series or an artist that you follow and really admire and would like to emulate. You may love the plot or the art and coloring, but it is that indefinable something else that sets a book apart and makes it truly memorable. If you analyze what that something is that makes you love a particular book, it may all boil down to the fact that you love the artist's graphic storytelling style. The truly great ones, like Jack Kirby or Adam Hughes, seem to be born with it, but good graphic storytelling techniques can most definitely be learned and nurtured. You may have read a million comics and graphic novels, but if you aren't aware of what is involved in telling the story and doing it with style, you should immediately take a hard analytical look at your favorites and break down what makes them tick, what drives the story, and what appeals to you in particular.

Chances are you have already started this process, and if you have, well and good. The next step is to do a pencil layout or dummy, where you can rough out the flow of the story quickly in thumbnail form, thereby working out any problems of pacing and ensuring your story fills the required pages effectively without going over or under the page count. This may be a bit daunting at first, but remember, it can done very quickly and with no need to expend much effort executing the art.

Styles are often a matter of taste, but the principles of good drafting and storytelling should never be compromised. This page from *Paladin Alpha* represents highly stylistic work that does not cross the line into self-indulgence.

Art by Matt Roberts, *Paladin Alpha* © 2006 Mark Ellis.

It is so integral to producing a good book that you shouldn't skip this stage. Remember, this stage is about planning, not your drafting! Check out **www.make shiftmiracle.com/TutTN.html** for a good tutorial on thumbnails.

When this stage is completed, only then can you begin in earnest on your pages, and at this point, of course, you should be doing so with the utmost care. Before you begin, read up on a couple of art topics in the following sections.

Anatomy and Perspective

If you are reading this book and seriously considering producing a graphic novel, we presume that you have had some experience and basic training in art. Having said this, we also are aware that the degree of training and experience of artists can vary greatly, so in the interests of giving an extra boost to those who may need it, we will briefly talk about the groundwork of any graphic storyteller's art: anatomy and perspective. They are part of the world-building skills necessary to create the background.

Lakota © 2006 Mark Ellis.

The following is a list of moderately priced books for beginners on human anatomy:

- *Drawing the Head and Figure* by Jack Hamm
- *The Figure: The Classic Approach to Drawing and Construction* by Walt Reed
- *How to Draw Comics the Marvel Way* by Stan Lee and John Buscema
- *How to Draw the Human Figure: Famous Artists School, Step-by-Step Method* by Cortina Famous Schools Staff
- *Dynamic Anatomy: Revised and Expanded Edition* by Burne Hogarth
- *Dynamic Figure Drawing* by Burne Hogarth

Even if you think you're pretty darn good, a few minutes spent on any book by Burne Hogarth is a good investment of time. Most of the acknowledged giants of the industry used Hogarth's books as unofficial training manuals.

Another resource is the Web, where many Web sites dealing with anatomy and proportion can be found. Check out the tutorials at **www.blazedent.com**.

When it comes to perspective, here are some recommendations:

- *Perspective Made Easy* by Ernest Norling
- *Perspective! For Comic Book Artists: How to Achieve a Professional Look in Your Artwork* by David Chelsea
- *Creative Perspective for Artists and Illustrators* by Ernest W. Watson
- *Perspective Drawing* by Kenneth W. Auvil

What all these books have in common is their accessibility and moderate price. They contain invaluable information for beginners but also tons of reference material and information for more experienced artists. It is important to start building a library of educational and reference materials to further hone your skills.

Art by Rik Levins, *Death Hawk* © 2006 Mark Ellis.

⚪ This page from *Death Hawk: The Soulworm Saga* showcases several perspectives from different angles.

Paladin Alpha © 2006 Mark Ellis.

🔺 Artist Matt Roberts depicted characters that were not only unique but also extremely expressive.

🔻 Meticulous attention to background detail makes this panel from *Death Hawk: The Soulworm Saga* memorable.

Expressive Characters

The story may be compelling with lots of action, the art may be interesting, and the lettering and coloring eye catching, but if your characters all look alike or have no capacity to convey emotion, you will lose your readers very quickly.

Everyone wants to relate to, understand, or be intrigued by the actors in a play; the same principle holds true for characters in a graphic novel. The lead characters must be distinctive, expressive, and individualistic or the reader simply doesn't care and stops turning the page. Try to think about the connections that readers might make to your characters.

Art by Rik Levins and Robert Lewis, © 2006 Mark Ellis.

I HAVE BUSINESS WITH AN EXECUTIVE.

MR. TAKUAN REQUESTED A SCHEMATIC OF THE PARTICLE ACCELERATOR.

MR. TAKUAN IS ENTERTAINING A WOMAN. SO BE DISCREET.

E-FACT

TODAY'S PENCILERS SEEM TO PREFER DRAWING VERY DETAILED PAGES, KNOWN AS TIGHT PENCILING, WITH EVERYTHING THEY WANT TO SEE IN THE INKED VERSION RENDERED IN GREAT DETAIL. THIS LEAVES LESS ROOM FOR INTERPRETATION BY THE INKER. IN THE EARLY DAYS QUITE FREQUENTLY ARTISTS WOULD USE THE LOOSE PENCILING APPROACH, WHICH ALLOWED THE INKER GREATER FREEDOM IN INTERPRETING THE PENCILER'S WORK.

Well-drawn facial expression and body language help immerse the reader in your imaginary world. Readers want to go there, and they are eager to see characters evolve and grow over the course of time or within a story arc.

So how do you carry that off? By really caring about the characters and their world. If you're not the scripter, collaborate with him to flesh out who the people are, what they believe in and stand for, and what they were inspired or damaged by in their lives up to this point. You must know their back story and their secrets to portray them with any accuracy or subtlety.

CHAPTER 10

LETTERER'S REQUIREMENTS

What to do, what to do! Should you use traditional hand lettering for your graphic novel or embrace the new computer lettering technology? In this chapter you'll read about the many angles and aspects and pros and cons of old versus new in the field of comics lettering. In Chapter 6 you briefly read about the importance of lettering to the overall appeal of your graphic novel project. This chapter gets down to the particulars and discusses in depth what is required for the letterer to do the job well, whether she is a hand letterer or computer letterer.

Typography in History

General knowledge of the history of lettering and type is helpful for the beginning letterer. Respect and admiration for this rich and complex artform comes from the knowledge that it began long before the advent of movable type and printing, when all books and documents had to be made by hand. Over time, different versions of fonts evolved that expressed mood and tone more accurately. After all, type is meant to stand for the spoken word, and to properly convey visually the cues we would normally pick up by ear we need bold type to give emphasis and italic type to make words stand apart and be noticed. From these sprang demibold and all-caps versions of fonts. Over the years, useful rules evolved concerning letterforms, which were then incorporated into the printing process and the mechanical evolution of handwriting into fonts. Font styles that conveyed mood and feeling while maintaining legibility were designed, and although these creations served a function and had practical applications, they were also a respected artform reserved for highly skilled craftsmen.

Letterers must have a good sense of space and design. They must be able to convey voice and feeling, shouting and whispering, accents and every permutation of the human voice, not to mention sound effects, while still fitting all the writer's wordy prose and dialogue into the space provided. Of course, if you're wearing all the hats, more than likely you'll be considerate of yourself and keep your word count down while leaving plenty of empty space for the word balloons. If you don't, after all, you'll have no one to blame but yourself!

▲ Fonts can be incredibly varied and express almost any mood.

An examination of ancient manuscripts, like Ireland's *Book of Kells*, shows an almost superhuman control of the pen, or actually, quill. The lettering is small, intricate, and precise; it is also almost impossibly regular and straight. The fantastical creatures and art depicted in that volume and other similar ones from that time period were so beautifully executed it is apparent that the monks who created these ancient books had a great love for the graphic arts, which leads us to our next section.

E-FACT

THE LATE, GREAT WILL EISNER WAS NOT ONLY A MASTER STORYTELLER AND ARTIST, HE ALSO WAS A MASTER LETTERER WHO PERFECTLY REPRESENTED HIS CHARACTERS IN THEIR WORD AND THOUGHT BALLOONS. EACH CHARACTER SPOKE IN A SLIGHTLY DIFFERENT FONT AND THE BALLOONS PERFECTLY FILLED THE SPACE. IN FACT, THE ANNUAL EISNER AWARDS INCLUDE A BEST LETTERER CATEGORY.

Hand Lettering

Do you have experience with calligraphy or hand lettering? If so, you're in luck, since you more than likely have the skills necessary to be a letterer without the assistance of a computer. Indeed, if you're technically challenged, hand lettering may be your only option. But that's okay; as you just learned, lettering has a long and respected history.

It also provides a very individualized and quirky result, as well as saving the many hundreds of dollars the computer letterer has to invest in the various tools of the trade: computer, monitor, graphics software, scanner, drawing tablet.

When tackling a project of graphic novel magnitude with its high page count, the letterer must strive to hone her skills or have had some experience already. If you do not, you must devote yourself to mastering the form through many hours of practice and with the help of tutorials and instructional materials.

Fortunately, if you're tackling the lettering duties and know you should brush up on your skills, there are many online resources available that can offer helpful advice and some preliminary steps to help prepare you for the task. Gather the materials you'll need and do your research. Try *http://members.shaw.ca/creatingcomics/lettering* for some helpful lettering advice.

Tools for Letterers

The Ames guide has been used by letterers, architects, and calligraphers, who have found it an invaluable tool for generations. It is still in use today, though not so much as in the past. Always used in conjunction with a T-square, this plastic tool with a rotating disk with holes for your pencil tip or lead costs less than four dollars.

It is used to draw parallel lines, which serve as guides for letter height, and for the space between lines of type, which is known in typography as the *leading*. It can at first glance be a puzzling and tricky instrument. The printed instructions are confusing, so unless you're a mechanical genius, it requires a demonstration of its operation for first-time users. Get the person in the art supply store to show you how to use it, or go online. There's a short, downloadable video at ***http://academics.triton. edu/faculty/jhalpin/ARC109/lecture_week_two.html***. Also, there's a good explanation of the process for lettering with the Ames Lettering Guide at ***www.blambot.com/handlettering.shtml***.

▲ The Ames Lettering Guide can make the life of a hand letterer a lot easier.

Additional tools that are needed by hand letterers can do double duty if you happen to be the penciler, colorist, and inker as well. Set up your workspace with:

- A drafting table
- Clip-on light
- T-square
- Ames Lettering Guide

- Oval templates
- French curve
- Technical pencil and sharpener
- Technical pens: .05 and .70 Rapidographs, Speedball B6 or C6, Micron 03 or 05 pens, Staedtler 03 sketch pens, and a Pigma Micron 08
- Hunt Crow Quill #107 or #102
- Eraser and eraser shield
- Ink: Higgins Engrossing or Speedball Superblack
- Artwork and tape
- Whiteout

One way to handle the workflow in the hand-lettering process is to letter directly on the penciled pages. Once the lettering is completed, along with sound effects, titles, and credits, it will go on to the inker. Another method is to letter on vellum overlays over photocopies or even the original art. The lettering can then be combined with the art after inking by the printing company, or it can be scanned and added to the scanned art digitally by either you or a service provider.

Either method starts with the letterer sitting down at her drafting table and drawing the horizontal guide lines by using an Ames Lettering Guide, a T-square, and a pencil. The Ames guide's evenly spaced holes allow you to choose the size you wish to use. Most letterers use a 3 or 4 setting. After the lettering has been penciled in, it is inked with a fine point tech pen and the balloon and caption borders are drawn. Lastly, the sound effects, captions, or titles are added as needed.

Computer Lettering Overview

If you're computer-savvy and your hand-lettering skills are minimal, there is still hope for you. Today, more comics and graphic novels are computer lettered than ever before, and the good news is there is a lot of information out there to assist the beginning letterer. There are sites that offer lettering fonts that convey the look of hand lettering without the years of practice and expertise it used to require to achieve that effect.

Death Hawk © 2006, Mark Ellis.

> A FEW GENERATIONS AGO, THE *HAWKEN* .690 WAS ONE OF THE MOST *DEVASTATING* FIREARMS EVER FORGED BY THE HANDS OF TERRANS.

▲ An example of hand lettering by Rik Levins, showing italics and boldface for emphasis.

Some folks argue that this digital-age shortcut undermines letterers and is somewhat akin to cheating, but they are shoveling against the tide. If your lettering skills are poor and you can't afford to hire a professional to do the job, computer lettering offers a viable and affordable option.

An early pioneer in computer lettering, British letterer Richard Starkings (*Batman: The Killing Joke*) made the switch from pen to computer in 1992 and never looked back. He's been quoted as saying, "If I never have to letter a page of a comic book with a pen ever again, I'll die a happy man."

Individuality need not be lost in the process; the truly creative letterer can opt to create fonts that mimic handwriting using Fontographer or similar font creation software. Graphic designer Deirdre DeLay designed a font (named Deirdre) that was used in many publications, such as *Doc Savage*, *Anne Rice's The Mummy*, and *The Miskatonic Project* books to speed up the production process.

There are many software packages that can be used to produce good digital lettering, including Photoshop, Illustrator, QuarkXPress, Macromedia FreeHand, and many others. The program you choose is entirely up to you. If you have already invested in one or more of these programs, you know how expensive they are and probably already have some experience in using them and know their capabilities. If you don't have any of the above, the people at *www.inkscape.org* offer a free program that they say is similar to Illustrator, Freehand, and CorelDraw.

Actual production procedures and technical requirements will vary according to your final choice of output provider, whether you are going to a commercial printer, a print-on-demand shop, or simply doing an online version of your book.

◀ On this page from *Death Hawk: The Soulworm Saga*, all of the dialogue balloons have been positioned and balanced correctly.

Death Hawk © 2006, Mark Ellis. Art by Rik Levins and Robert Lewis.

Most definitely in all cases you should talk to your supplier's prepress and production people to verify all technical requirements. The ultimate goal is to get correctly positioned type, word balloons, sound effects, and so on onto the page, and all of these programs will do that.

When you have made that choice, resources are abundant online and in print for detailed production procedures. The folks at Balloon Tales talk about the advantages of using Adobe Illustrator for lettering (*www.balloontales .com/articles/beginners/software.html*). They also discuss software needed for other steps in the production process.

A great online source of information on page composition and lettering in QuarkX-Press can be found at *www.balloontales.com/tips/ quark/index.html*. This is a page linked to the Comicraft Web site, *www.comicbookfonts.com/home .html?sid=0001EDJrBQfleugW2U4j6Q*, which not only has downloadable fonts (for a fee) but also contains a wealth of information about the lettering process, including a glossary of terms at *www.balloontales.com/articles/glossary/index.html*.

An index of sites with lettering tutorials can be found at: *http://hans.presto.tripod.com/links005 .html*.

For Macromedia Freehand fans, *http://hans .presto.tripod.com/glumace_primer.html* has an overview of the procedure for that program.

Another source of comics fonts that are free and downloadable can be found at Blambot: *www.blambot.com/fonts.shtml*. This site also has quite a selection of commercial comics fonts available, too. These aren't free, but they are immediately downloadable. Fonts are available for both Macs and PCs, and you can download and install the free font, A.C.M.E. Secret Agent, on your hard drive in no time. Be sure to choose a font that has a regular, bold, and italic version in order to properly express a range of emotions. Suggested reading for letterers can be found in:

- *DC Comics Guide to Coloring and Lettering Comics* by Mark Chiarello and Todd Klein
- *Comic Book Lettering: The Comicraft Way* by Richard Starkings
- *Digital Prepress for Comic Books: The Definitive Desktop Production Guide* by Kevin Tinsley
- *The Complete Calligrapher* by Frederick Wong

E-FACT

KEEP IN MIND THAT IF YOU ARE DOING ALL THE PRODUCTION ON A PROJECT YOURSELF, CHOOSE SOFTWARE PROGRAMS THAT WILL MEET ALL YOUR NEEDS AS A SCANNER, COLORIST, AND LETTERER AS WELL. THIS MAY REQUIRE BUYING ILLUSTRATOR, PHOTOSHOP, AND QUARKXPRESS OR PAGEMAKER. EXPERIENCE IS THE BEST TEACHER, SO CHECK AROUND FOR THE LATEST WORD ON THE TOPIC.

Here is a list of the basic tools you'll need for computer lettering:

- ❑ Mac or PC computer
- ❑ Large monitor
- ❑ Graphics software, such as MS Word, Adobe Photoshop, Illustrator, InDesign, Freehand, PageMaker, or QuarkXPress
- ❑ Digital drawing tablet
- ❑ Scanner

Sound Effects, Captions, and Dialogue Balloons

Thanks to the *Batman* TV show from the 1960s, some people still associate comic books with gigantic sound effects such as POW!, BAM!, and SPLAT!

The overdone display lettering in comics was adopted by the pop art movement of the '60s and '70s.Comics-related pieces by Roy Lichtenstein and Andy Warhol were viewed by critics as symbolizing the inherent absurdity of the form.

E-FACT

A SUBGENRE OF COMIC BOOKS GREW FROM THE "BWAHAHAH!" SOUND EFFECT. THIS SOUND EFFECT DATES BACK TO THE 1980S AND KEITH GIFFEN AND J.M. DEMATTEIS'S RUN ON *JUSTICE LEAGUE*, WHERE IT BECAME A RUNNING JOKE FOR CHARACTERS TO LAUGH USING THE "BWAHAHAH!" SOUND EFFECT. OVER THE YEARS IT DEVELOPED INTO A PARODY OF THE MORE ABSURD ASPECTS OF THE SUPERHERO GENRE.

Art by Adam Hughes and Dan McKinnon, *Death Hawk* © 2006 Mark Ellis.

▲ This panel from *Death Hawk: The Soulworm Saga* is dominated by a giant sound effect, rendered by letterer Dan McKinnon.

▶ In this sequence from *Ninja Elite*, artist and letterer Franc Reyes balances action and sound effects perfectly.

During that period, Marvel Comics embraced the pop art culture (for a time their covers carried the Marvel Pop-Art Productions banner), and their books were filled with pages upon pages of giant sound effects such as THOOM! and B-TANG!

Although sound effects are definitely part of the comics tradition, a number of artists do not care for them or use them very sparingly. Writers are usually responsible for coming up with sound effects. In my experience, I think that they often enhance the storytelling, but there is no denying they can be overused or overdone.

One way letterers can make sound effects blend in with the art is to design the actual words to symbolize the sound, such as rendering KA-BOOM! in an explosive style as if the letters themselves are shaking or blowing apart.

However, always be conscious of how the text, display lettering included, blends with the art. The placement of balloons and captions in a panel is crucial. When the reader becomes involved with the story, then the shape and size of the balloons and the caption boxes should be part of the image and be so unobtrusive that they are unconsciously accepted.

CHAPTER 11

INKER'S REQUIREMENTS

The job of the inker is tricky and sometimes thankless. If the final product looks good the penciler gets the credit, but if the work looks bad the inker may take a lot of the blame. Many pencilers prefer to ink their own pencils or use an inker they have worked with before whose work they know and trust. An inker's style can either enhance or harm the underlying pencil work, so before tackling this demanding job, be sure you're armed with the right tools and knowledge.

Interpreting the Pencils

Inking and penciling were not always separate tasks. Artists used to ink over their own pencils more often than not after laying them out in an unfinished way. Comics publishers soon realized this was not conducive to producing art on a timely basis. Deciding to assign two people to split the art chores and effectively cut the production time in half was a pretty efficient idea, especially in the boom years of comics' so-called golden age.

What You Need

Inking is not just tracing the pencilers' work with India ink using a pen or brush. It requires a serious artist with a high degree of hand-eye coordination and a good deal of artistic ability who can stay true to the penciler's work yet enhance the smaller details. Not all inkers are good artists, but a good inker can save the work of an amateur penciler by correcting anatomical or perspective problems. This is called *finalizing*. If you are creating your own graphic novel, you will more than likely have a great deal of control over the inking process.

Image © 2006 Mark Ellis.

▲ This loose pencil rendering by Don Heck was finalized by inker Robert Lewis.

A close collaboration between the penciler and inker is the ideal way to ensure a final product that remains faithful to the original vision. Without the pressure of a regular monthly comic's production schedule, it is perfectly feasible for one person to handle both penciling and inking chores.

The inker's needs as far as tools, supplies, and setup are similar to those of both the penciler and letterer:

- A drafting table or flat work surface
- Clip-on light
- T-square
- Two #2 Windsor-Newton sable brushes; the first for black ink, the second for corrections in white ink or gouache
- Mars Staedtler sketch pens
- Hunt No. #102 Crow Quill nib pen
- White plastic eraser and eraser shield
- Higgins Black Magic India Ink by Sanford
- Whiteout or white gouache
- Q-tips for laying down solid black areas

Digital Inking

It was inevitable that if more and more tasks are being taken over by computers that inking might be, too. Some say the biggest drawback to the process is that digital inking looks rather like high-contrast pencils; nonetheless, it seems apparent that digital inking is a trend that will probably gain traction more and more as time goes by and mastering the software necessary to do it will become simpler and cheaper.

Currently, studios that do both inking and coloring digitally are getting more and more work. For more information as to the process and equipment needed to do digital inking, check out Brian Haberlin's *Digital Art Tutorials: Digital Inking Volume 1* CD-ROM. Haberlin's coloring studio has been responsible for thousands of digitally colored comic book pages, including *Spawn*, *Spider-Man*, *The Incredible Hulk*, *Uncanny X-Men*, and more.

E-FACT

GOLDEN AGE COMICS ARTIST LOU FINE (CAPTAIN MARVEL, JR.) WAS FAMOUS FOR BEING ABLE TO RENDER A FAR THINNER INK LINE WITH A SABLE BRUSH THAN OTHER INKERS WERE ABLE TO MANAGE WITH THE SHARPEST OF CROW QUILL PENS. SOME HAVE SPECULATED THAT THE TERM *FINE LINE* DERIVES FROM HIS PRACTICE.

The digital inker should probably first have experience in real-world inking. In addition, not surprisingly, you'll also need a computer with tons of memory, at least a gigabyte of RAM. You'll also need a large monitor with 1024 x 768 minimum resolution, a scanner, a drawing tablet, vector-based drawing software such as Adobe Illustrator or CorelDRAW, and image manipulation software such as Adobe Photoshop.

Death Hawk © 2006 Mark Ellis.

Death Hawk © 2006 Mark Ellis.

Good, tight pencils help too, and some digital inkers prep the page and clean it up a bit before scanning the art in at 600 dpi, usually in bitmap mode. The big advantage to digital inking is that if you make a mistake it's a snap to undo it and move on. Also, if you're wearing the colorist's hat as well, you will already have the pages scanned and ready to be colorized. It isn't necessarily faster than conventional inking, but it is an option you might think about exploring, particularly if you already have the computer setup and software.

Online resources for digital inkers include *www.renderosity.com/mod/tutorial/index.php?tutorial_id=1552* and *http://apps.corel.com/painterix/training/tutorial_inking.html?trkid=tpc1006ft*.

Respecting the Line

You've already read about the responsibilities of an inker, but it's worth noting again the importance of respecting the penciler's vision when inking the project. An inker who takes liberties and either adds too much or ignores important details is an inker who isn't taking the work seriously. Respect the line, respect the penciler's intent, and in return your work will be respected as well.

What does respecting the line mean? It means following the pencils as much as possible and consulting with the penciler if there is any confusion as to intent. Pencilers and inkers should share a common vision, since they are working as a team and it is a collaboration.

That said, there are inkers so good at their jobs that they can take the sketchiest pencils and embellish them to such a degree that they make the art outstanding, and they do this without taking anything away from the original. These inkers usually started out as pencilers and are excellent draftsmen in their own right. They know anatomy, proportion, and perspective and have the self-assurance to add appropriate detail when necessary. The inker's job is to bring the writer and penciler's vision to life. Some effects and lighting are difficult to convey with pencils, but a good inker can make them seem real. They very much are in control of how mood, lighting, movement, and texture are conveyed to the reader.

E-FACT

FAMED SPIDER-MAN ARTIST JOHN ROMITA BROKE INTO COMICS PRETENDING TO INK FOR A PENCILER WHO WAS ACTUALLY INKING ROMITA'S PENCILS. IN AN INTERVIEW THAT APPEARED IN ALTER EGO MAGAZINE #9, ROMITA TOLD INTERVIEWER ROY THOMAS THAT HE STARTED OUT WORKING FOR ARTIST LESTER ZAKARIN, WHO PRETENDED TO STAN LEE TO BE PENCILING MATERIAL THAT ROMITA INKED, WHEREAS THE TRUTH OF THE SITUATION WAS THE OPPOSITE.

A number of famed comic artists relied heavily on collaborations with inkers to make their work stand out. Jim Mooney, an accomplished penciler in his own right, finalized John Romita's work on *Spider-Man* for many years. Inker Joe Sinnott polished and finalized Jack Kirby's pencils on the *Fantastic Four*, and Murphy Anderson enhanced Curt Swan's pencils on *Superman* for a number of years.

While inking involves tracing the pencil lines, it also requires interpreting the pencils, giving proper weight to the lines, correcting mistakes, and making other creative choices. The final look of a penciler's finished work can vary enormously depending on the skills of the individual inkers.

Paladin Alpha © 2006 Mark Ellis.

🔺 Darryl Banks indicated on his pencil rendering of the *Paladin Alpha* cover where he wanted inker Chris Leidenfrost to spot the blacks.

▶ Inker Bob Lewis used a variety of different line weights to embellish Don Heck's architectural details in this page from *The Miskatonic Project: The Whisperer in Darkness.*

Good inkers do more than simply interpret the pencil lines into pen and brush strokes. Depending on the amount of detail the penciler puts into the original drawings, the inker might find himself acting like a motion picture lighting expert—adding shade or placing black areas (known as *spotting blacks*) and shadows in the final drawing.

Many pencilers will mark their art with a series of *X*s to indicate to the inker the areas to be filled with black. Not all pencilers do this—very often they prefer to shade in all the areas that they want to be black—but this can be an impediment since the buildup of graphite interferes with the absorption of ink.

Often it can be up to the inker to determine the direction of the light source. This is important since the direction dictates where the shift of the line weight will be. For example, if the light falls upon a character or an object from the right, then the weight of the line will be thinner on the light side and heavier in the dark direction. Varying the weight or thickness of the ink line is a common practice in high-contrast artwork. Keep in mind that almost all of the rules of penciling apply to inking as well.

To tell a story, the art must be clear and convincing, and sometimes it may fall upon the inker to enhance a certain sequence with force or speed lines to add dynamism to what could be a static panel. At one time Zipatone (grey areas of different textures on clear adhesive film) was popular among inkers to give the art an added sense of depth and dimension.

Image and *The Miskatonic Project* © 2006 Mark Ellis.

An experienced inker will use different techniques to suggest different settings and textures, such as crosshatching with a pen point or feathering with a brush or crow quill. The appropriate placement of blacks and lines can delineate everything from bricks to scales to shadows.

Some inkers prefer to use brushes exclusively, since they feel it gives them more control over the fluidity and line weight. Other inkers prefer pens, but most inkers prefer a mixture of the two, going back and forth with different combinations until they achieve the desired effect.

A seldom used, very labor-intensive technique that can produce beautiful effects is stippling. In this approach, the inker uses a pen point to make small dots on the page to give the image a tonal range from solid black to white.

▶ Robert Lewis's inks over Don Heck's pencils show the detail that the inker can bring to a page. Note the bricks, facial shadows, linework, and crosshatching.

Another technique is gray wash, using ink-diluted water to give a wide range of gray tones. This method is usually reserved for books printed in black and white.

An experienced inker teamed with a novice penciler can correct anatomical errors, alter facial expressions, or even improve the artwork in a variety of other ways. Conversely, a novice inker can ruin the work of even the most accomplished penciler.

E-FACT

PROFESSIONAL INKERS HAVE BEEN KNOWN TO USE MANY DIFFERENT KINDS OF ITEMS TO ACHIEVE CERTAIN KINDS OF SPECIAL EFFECTS. OLD, WORN-OUT BRUSHES CAN EMULATE LEAFY TREE BRANCHES, AND INK-SOAKED Q-TIPS ARE GOOD FOR RENDERING PLUMES OF SMOKE. OLD TOOTHBRUSHES WERE FAVORITE TOOLS OF JACK KIRBY.

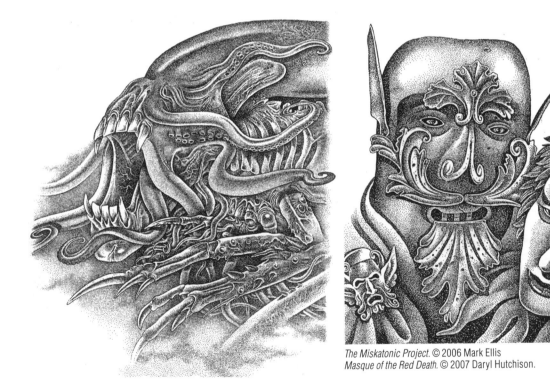

The Miskatonic Project. © 2006 Mark Ellis
Masque of the Red Death. © 2007 Daryl Hutchison.

▲ Artist Daryl Hutchinson used the stippling technique to achieve a unique effect in these illustrations from *The Miskatonic Project: The Whisperer in Darkness* and *Masque of the Red Death.*

Ninja Elite © 2006 Mark Ellis.

⏺ Artist Franc Reyes used a gray wash to ink his own pencils in *Ninja Elite*, by Franc Reyes and Mark Ellis.

Many artists are renowned for their *tight* pencils, basically turning in a finished piece of work that could almost be printed without being inked. Other artists prefer much looser work, particularly if they intend to ink themselves. Veterans such as Jim Mooney and Don Heck often inked their own work, in which case they would basically just sketch out the pencil lines.

The division between penciler and inker described here is most frequently found where the penciler and inker are hired independently of each other by the publisher. In the instance of an artist hiring his own inkers, the roles are less structured. Milton Caniff, for example, inked all the faces of the characters while leaving the assistant to ink the backgrounds and secondary figures. Like penciling, inking is a very specialized skill, and just as with penciling, it might take months, if not years, of practice before you're proficient.

COLORIST'S REQUIREMENTS

Artistic necessity drives coloring, whether it's done with Dr. Martin's Dyes, as it was formerly, or with the help of a sophisticated computer system and software. The skills required to be a colorist today have not changed much, although the new technology is now cheaper and more accessible. Little respect was given to colorists back in the days when flat color was laid in on the page, but today's colorists can and do create a nuanced world that affects mood and tone, perhaps even more than the inker's work does.

Computer Coloring Process

As technology grows more accessible and affordable, the practicality of coloring comics by hand decreases every year. Eventually it may become a lost art. Computer coloring has another advantage: It can generate color separations, which saves both time and money.

You Can Do It

If you have some color sense and an art background, plus the proper computer setup, you can learn to color your work on the computer. Allow yourself time to practice the program and learn the process. Gaining proficiency in Photoshop and other coloring software can take some time. Good tutorials and books are a great way to learn. The Internet has tons of materials to help you out. The Adobe Web site can help you master the basic tools of Photoshop or Elements, plus it has tutorials to help you out. Adobe Photoshop is the image-processing software of choice for most colorists, yet some use other programs such as Corel's Painter.

The New Justice Machine © 2006 Mark Ellis.

⬤ This splash page from *The Justice Machine* was originally hand colored with Dr. Martin's Dyes by Deirdre DeLay. The tonal qualities and coverage are very different than what can be achieved with computer coloring programs.

Art by Adam Hughes, Deirdre DeLay color artist. *Death Hawk* © 2006 Mark Ellis.

⬤ This page from *Death Hawk: The Soulworm Saga* was colored on the computer using Adobe Photoshop.

Currently, computers are affordable and within the reach of most people, and artists on a budget no longer have to use pricey Mac systems to do their production; most graphics programs are now available for PCs as well. Graphics files saved as JPEGs or TIFFs on either machine can be burned onto a CD or DVD or even sent over a high-speed Internet connection to printers and color separators.

That's the good news. The bad news is that it's still rather pricey to get the proper setup to scan, clean up, and color your page files. A suggested setup might consist of:

- A computer with 512 MB–2 GB of RAM and at least a 60 GB hard drive
- As large a monitor as you can afford
- A scanner that can scan up to 600 dpi
- Photoshop, Photoshop Elements, or Painter
- An inkjet printer
- A Wacom or equivalent drawing tablet
- An Internet connection

An Overview of the Process

This quick overview gives a look at one of the ways that colorists use to create professional-quality coloring. Black-and-white line art is scanned at 600 dpi as a bitmap image then converted to grayscale and cleaned up to ensure that the lines are crisp and black and that any specks or gray tints are removed.

This can be done with a combination of levels adjustments, contrast adjustments, and the eraser and brush tools. Some colorists at this point will create an alpha channel and fill it with black. This is accomplished by going to the channels palette and creating new channels. (See details in Chris Arlidge's tutorial referenced in the following list.)

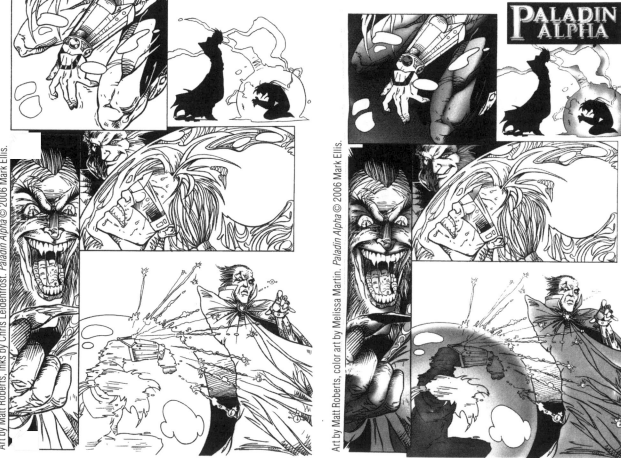

Art by Matt Roberts, inks by Chris Leidenfrost. *Paladin Alpha* © 2006 Mark Ellis.

Art by Matt Roberts, color art by Melissa Martin. *Paladin Alpha* © 2006 Mark Ellis.

▲ An inked page of *Paladin Alpha* scanned at 600 dpi in preparation for computer coloring.

▲ The same page from *Paladin Alpha* after a restrained palette of colors has been applied in Photoshop.

Other colorists choose "Multiply" and make layers transparent to facilitate dropping color into large areas. (See Sara Turner's tutorial referenced in the following list.) Save the image as your file backup. Most colorists downsize their images to 300 dpi to reduce the file size of the page. There are some exceptions to this, but in most instances a 300 dpi image is totally appropriate.

Check out these sites and books to get an overview of the process from different color artists:

- Artist Chris Arlidge has a seventeen-step coloring tutorial:
  www.steeldolphin-forums.com/htmltuts/digital_ colorpart2.html
- Artist Howard Cruse's Web site:
  www.howardcruse.com/howardsite/feature6/ coloringcomics/index.html
- From Sara Turner, a good tutorial (click on: A Comics Color Tutorial—Sara Turner):
  http://mlatcomics.com/phpBB2/viewforum.php?f=9
- This Antarctic Press Web site has publications and CDs for sale devoted to coloring regular comics and manga:
  www.antarcticpress.com/html/version_01/store .php?id=How+To+Color+Comics
- *How to Color for Comics* by Guru eFX:
  www.guru-efx.com
- *The DC Comics Guide to Coloring and Lettering Comics* by Mark Chiarello and Todd Klein
- *Beginner's Guide to Coloring Comics Using the Computer* by Dudley Bryan, Jr.

E-FACT

IN *THE HULK* #1, THE TITLE CHARACTER'S SKIN WAS COLORED GRAY RATHER THAN THE GREEN HE HAS BEEN ASSOCIATED WITH FOR THE LAST FORTY PLUS YEARS. A STABLE SHADE OF GRAY COULDN'T BE MAINTAINED THROUGHOUT THE ISSUE; THEREFORE, STAN LEE MADE THE DECISION TO CHANGE THE HULK'S SKIN COLOR TO A LESS TROUBLESOME GREEN.

Flatting is a term color artists use for the process of filling the page with large areas of solid color that are tweaked later. This process can be quickly mastered if you know the basics of Photoshop. Some color production studios have assistants who do all the flatting and someone who finishes their work, filling in detailed areas such as faces and areas with highlights and shadows and where required adding more detail and sophistication to the overall image without harming the underlying pixels. Check out the flats tutorial at *www.mart inity.com/html/tutorials/flats/flats.htm*. GutterZombie's Forum has tips and tricks from comics professionals at *www.dave-co.com/gutterzombie/*.

Painters' Sensibility and Color Context

Nobody becomes wealthy by coloring comics, and comic colorists get little respect even though their work has such a huge impact on the look and mood of the finished book. For some reason, perhaps just ignorance of the whole process, there is the perception that coloring comics is easy. It isn't. Whether you are a traditional or computer colorist, you must be an artist with a good sense of the impact of color on the reader. You are in essence a painter who gives the extra dimension of color to the page, allowing readers to immerse themselves more deeply in the book. The computer colorist also has special effects tricks up her sleeve unavailable to hand colorists.

Art by Jim Mooney, *Lakota* © 2006 Mark Ellis.

▲ These black-and-white pages from *Lakota* can be compared to the same pages computer-colored by Melissa Martin in the color insert.

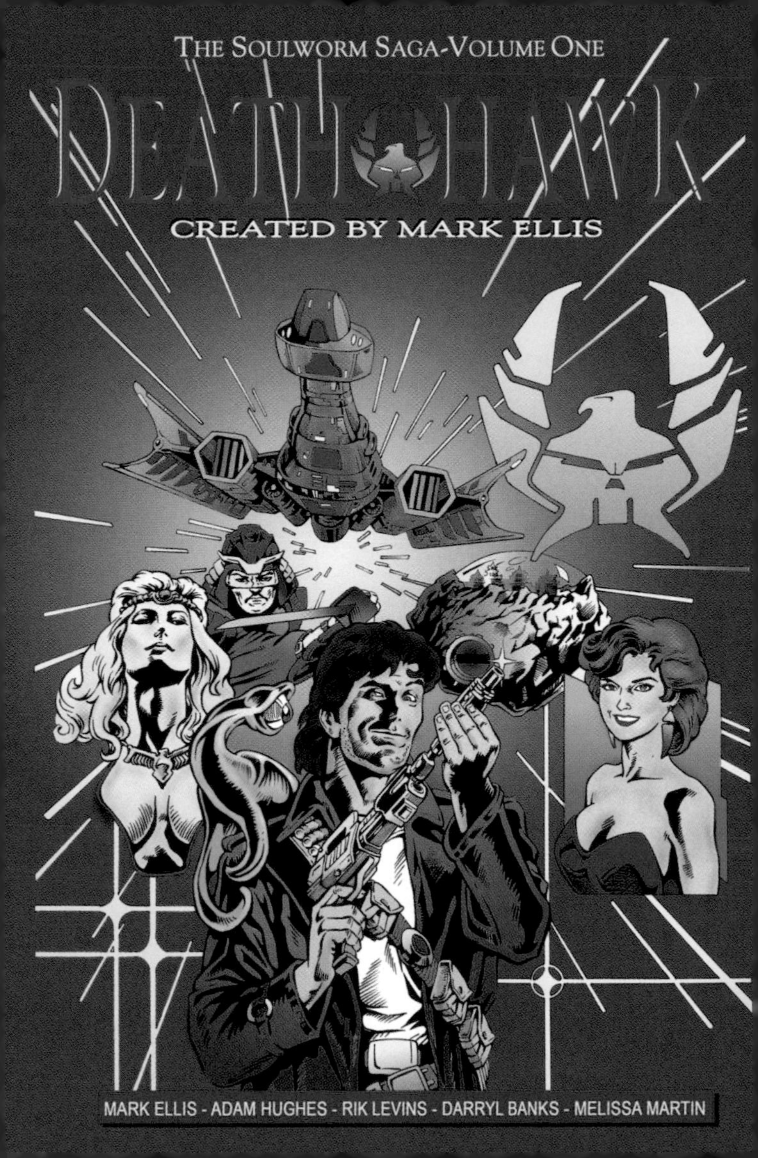
THE SOULWORM SAGA-VOLUME ONE
DEATHHAWK
CREATED BY MARK ELLIS
MARK ELLIS - ADAM HUGHES - RIK LEVINS - DARRYL BANKS - MELISSA MARTIN

Artist Paul Mounts advocates using the term *color artist* rather than *colorist,* remarking that semantics greatly influence people's perceptions of things. I think his observation is correct. It is high time to recognize the talent and sophistication of color in today's graphic novel market. Check out the color scheme tool available from Chris Arlidge at Steel Dolphin Creative Tools (**www.steeldolphin.com/color_scheme .html**). It is a fantastic design tool that can help you create a complementary, monochromatic, triadic, or analogic color scheme for the Web or in print. It is fun and simple to use. To be a good colorist you must be a painter, with all the talent and knowledge that entails. You may not have to know how to mix colors, but you do have to have good color sense and a firm grasp of what makes a page's color schemes work, where to lead the eye, and the restraint to do all this without overwhelming the inks.

Old School Hand Coloring

Today's comic creators are using computers almost exclusively to color their art. But as *Daredevil* color artist Matt Hollingsworth says, "Manually painting is a lot of fun, and I miss it sometimes. I think that those of us who started before digital was around actually have an edge on other folks, at least those of us who survived and made the transition. Knowing how to really paint with real paint can only be a good thing, and I think has helped me tremendously even in my digital work."

Hollingsworth graduated from the Kubert School in 1991, right as digital coloring was in its infancy. He raises a good point. In the earliest color comics, the process for getting tints onto the page was incredibly tedious, involving a coding system that the colorist notated onto a black-and-white photostat of the line art. For many years, the preferred method of coloring comics was by using acetate overlays—thin, transparent plastic sheets that accepted printing ink. Acetate was even used for the production of sequences in animated films. This was a very time-consuming, painstaking process requiring much more technical rather than artistic skill.

E-FACT

STEVE BUCCELLATO, COLORIST AND PUBLISHER OF COMICULTURE, MENTIONED IN AN INTERVIEW ON WWW.MANWITHOUTFEAR.COM THAT IN HIS OPINION, "THE ONLY DISADVANTAGE OF COMPUTER COLORING TAKING OVER THE BUSINESS IS THAT IT'S TAKEN WORK AWAY FROM SOME GOOD COLORISTS WHO AREN'T COMPUTER-SAVVY. UNFORTUNATELY, THE NEWER COLORISTS WHO HAVE REPLACED THE OLD ARE OFTEN NOT TRAINED IN THE MOST IMPORTANT ASPECTS OF COMIC BOOK COLORING: STORYTELLING AND CLARIFYING THE LINE ART. MOST OF THE NEW GUYS ARE TOO ENAMORED WITH THE TOOL AND NOT THE CRAFT."

The colors were made of percentages of each of the three primary colors, and the various combinations that could be mixed added up to a palette of sixty-four hues and tints, although most of them were never used. Shades of gray very often printed as black or even purple.

E-FACT

THE FIRST COMIC ARTIST TO COLOR HIS OWN WORK WAS RICHARD CORBEN WITH HIS DEN SAGA THAT APPEARED IN THE EARLY ISSUES OF *HEAVY METAL MAGAZINE*. WITH A PROCESS CAMERA, HE COMBINED PHOTOGRAPHIC AND HALFTONE TEXTURES WITH HIS LINE ART AND ACHIEVED A UNIQUE EFFECT.

Since the colors used in printing are cyan, magenta, yellow, and black (referred to as process colors), and percentages of these colors produce all other shades, the code for purple would reflect a mixture of red (magenta) and blue (cyan), perhaps 50 percent of each. The code for a purple cape would be indicated on the proof as R50B50. This method limited the colors to a selection of only sixty-four different colors and allowed for very little gradation in shading. An understanding of this will give you more appreciation of old comics, where it was painfully apparent at times how this process can go horribly wrong under rushed production schedules.

In the 1970s, DC artist Murphy Anderson, best known for his long stint as the penciler/inker on *Hawkman*, started Visual Concepts, a graphics company. They offered color separation services, and due to his expertise were able to increase the available palette to 128 colors.

The industry gradually moved away from this production method in the late '80s when Dr. Martin's Dyes, a permanent watercolor ink, came into use. This process allowed color to be applied directly to the page from which the color separations were then made. Dr. Martin's Dyes could also be used to do production in a manner similar to the gouache method, as they were designed to function as process colors as well.

E-QUESTION
WHAT ARE COLOR SEPARATIONS?

COLOR SEPARATIONS ARE REPRESENTATIONS OF THE IMAGE TO BE PRINTED BROKEN DOWN INTO THE PRIMARY COLORS CYAN, MAGENTA, AND YELLOW. WHEN BLACK IS ADDED, THESE FOUR COLORS CAN RECREATE A NEARLY UNLIMITED COLOR PALETTE ON A STANDARD FOUR-COLOR PRESS. EACH SINGLE-COLOR LAYER IS PRINTED, ONE ON TOP OF THE OTHER, AND CREATES WHAT LOOKS LIKE A FULL-COLOR IMAGE.

Art by Darryl Banks, *The New Justice Machine* © 2006 Mark Ellis.

Art by Darryl Banks, colors by Deirdre DeLay. *The Miskatonic Project* © 2006 Mark Ellis.

⬧ This page from *The New Justice Machine* was colored using the gouache method.

⬧ This cover from *The Miskatonic Project: The Whisperer in Darkness* was painted with Dr. Martin's Dyes.

European comic publishers had been printing full-color graphic albums for years using the blueline system. Using this method, the original art was copied in a nonreproducing blue onto artboard by a photochemical process. The color artist then painted on the blueline board. Another copy of the black line art was put onto clear acetate, which was used as an overlay so the colorists could see how the final product would look in print. The color was photographed separately to get clean colors, and the black was added as a separate plate. This gave a nice sharp look, but it was not a cheap method since it required photographic color separations and better paper.

In the 1990s, independent publishers who didn't have large print runs began painting their books, a process that involved making copies of the original inked art, then using Dr. Martin's Dyes directly on the copy. Color separations were then shot from these pages. Pages produced in this way had a very painterly look, as indeed they should have. All the effects achievable with brush and paint were available to the color artist without the clumsy, mechanical production process involved in the color-coded techniques. They were able to achieve full color rather than the flat, hand-separated, acetate-overlay system that was still in place at Marvel, DC, and Archie.

Artists were able to achieve subtle gradation in tone and variations in palettes not available to them formerly, and effects of greater subtlety and impact could be more easily achieved. Today, of course, computer colorists have an infinite palette of colors, hues, tints, and tones available to them.

CHAPTER 13

PRODUCTION FLOW CHART

Here is the part of a complicated artistic endeavor that every creative person tries to avoid—getting organized! You may be a multitalented combination of Shakespeare and da Vinci, and you may feel you have the whole project together conceptually, but eventually it all has to be put down on paper and planned in an orderly, step-by-step manner. Take a deep breath, grab a calendar and pen and paper, and start making your plans. This chapter will make this as painless as possible.

Script to Pencils

Since the script is the skeleton upon which the meat and muscle of the story hangs, it is at this stage that the writer and penciler, if they are not one and the same person, should get to know each other's strengths and weaknesses. The scripter and artist, and any other team members, should meet in person if possible; if not, phone or Internet communication will have to suffice. These days it is easy to collaborate over the Internet. With the help of instant message programs files can be quickly exchanged, and with voice-over-Internet-protocol (VoIP) technology you can even chat free.

The writer's plot should already be in a basic conceptual form. The pacing and high points of the story should be ready to be kicked around with the penciler. Be sure everyone at the planning meeting has a written copy of the plot to make notes on. The penciler should have a pen and pad handy in case a visual image comes to mind that needs to be conveyed to the scripter.

If your inker, letterer, and colorist are around, invite them to participate, too. This collaboration at such an early stage can yield amazing results. The story can be custom crafted to the artist's particular expertise.

```
PAGE FOUR:

Panel 1: CYKE speaks to HAWK, VANESSA in b.g. Ref. Page 23, panel 6.

CYKE(1): In some unknown manner, it appears that Ms. Bouvier has absorbed
the properties of the artifact.
        (2): In essence, she has become the artifact.

Panel 2: HAWK drags VANESSA to the stasis tube. Ref. Page 24, panel 3.

CAP(3): Even my patience had its limits.

HAWK(4): You can rest in the stasis tube 'til we reach our destination.
        (5): My client can sort this out.

Panel 3: Ext. view of PROGENETRIX. The PEREGRINE approaches it, soaring
between security satellites. Ref. Page 25, panel 5.

CAP(6): Progenetrix, the world housing the Biotech corporation was the
destination--

DEATH HAWK # 2 Reference starts here.

Panel 4: HAWK shakes hands with CHANE. Ref. Page 4, panel 4. Fairly large
panel, showing FREYA and the motto BUILDING A BETTER HUMANITY in the b.g.
Lots of neg. space.

CAP(7): And Biotech's C.E.O., Anton Chane, was my client.
        (8): Biotech builds Mimetic Extraterrans...known in local parlance
as "ME"'s...they're up to series 7 now. They're synthetic people.
Supposedly perfect people.
        (9): Everyone on Progenetrix looks like a god, and everyone there
makes my stomach turn.
```

⬥ An example of a script from *Death Hawk*, with a panel-by-panel breakdown, dialogue, and references to existing art. Scripts are often taped to the back of the actual art.

As mentioned in Chapter 6, a story that features imagery that the penciler is expert at depicting will be much more believable and interesting than one that does not play to his strengths.

GRAPHIC NOVEL FLOW CHART

	Jan.	Feb.	March	April	May	June	July	Aug.	Sep.	Oct.	Nov.	Dec.
Cover												
Promos												
Pencils												
Inks												
Scans												
Color												
Printer												
Ship Date												

◀ You can make your own chart to keep track of production stages.

The artist may also have some input as to interesting scenes to place in the story, including the planning of sound effects. The penciler can also do a reality check if the scripter is asking too much as far as depicting a scene goes. This is a good time for the penciler to speak up and tell the writer his honest reaction to the feasibility of completing the project satisfactorily.

E-FACT

DIGITAL PRINTING AND PRINT ON DEMAND WILL CHANGE THE FACE OF PUBLISHING IN THE NEAR FUTURE, AND THEY HOLD THE MOST PROMISE FOR SELF-PUBLISHING AND SMALL PRESS PROJECTS. SHORT-RUN PRINTINGS OF BLACK-AND-WHITE BOOKS HAVE REACHED AN AFFORDABLE PRICE, AND THERE IS UNDOUBTEDLY GOING TO BE A RAPID DROP IN THE COST OF COLOR PRINTING IN THE NEAR FUTURE AS TECHNOLOGY KEEPS IMPROVING.

At this stage of the book, the writer has presumably familiarized himself with the penciler's previous work, if not in printed form then at least in a portfolio.

If a script has been finalized, the penciler and writer should go over it at this point so that the artist clearly understands what the story is about, what the high points of it are, and what the writer wants to emphasize most. They should also discuss some ideas for splash pages and scenes of high drama and importance, as well as character design and overall mood and atmosphere. Exploring these issues at the very beginning ensures that the creators of the project are pulling together toward the same goal, not pulling against each other's vision of the book, which can stall or kill a project.

At this stage, all the nuts-and-bolts issues must be ironed out and agreed upon: scheduling, page rate, the shared responsibilities. Don't leave anything up in the air; this is the time to nail down and specify all details, preferably in writing. If you are handling both the script and penciling, most of these issues aren't pertinent with the exception of scheduling and writing down key issues.

Next, get out a calendar and set a deadline for completion of the project. Be realistic when considering how many pages you will have to finish per week to meet your goal. A commitment to a schedule will keep you on track and also can be an invaluable aid in helping to plan the later stages of the project when other members of the team are brought into play. This is also the stage at which you should start getting quotes from any service providers you plan on using, such as printers, color separators, or shippers.

Here's a checklist for the planning meeting:

❏ *Expectations*—Be clear as to what is expected from each team member and what the overarching goals are. What do they want individually as far as compensation? What level of sales are you aiming for?

❏ *Schedules and timelines*—Get a realistic assessment and step-by-step breakdown of how long it will take to complete each stage of the project.

❏ *Duties*—Determine who will scan the art; do the cover; design the logos; proofread the script and lettering; contact printers for quotes; issue press releases; handle shipping the books; do the ads, promotions, and flyers, apply for grants; examine proofs; mail out orders; and, last but not least, manage the launch party.

Pencils to Inks

When the first batch of pencils is completed to the satisfaction of both writer and penciler, it is time to start getting the pages to the inker. The pages can be exchanged in batches as they are completed. This is usually done by express mail or hand delivery. If your inker lives nearby, the collaboration is easier as the penciler can give immediate feedback and answer any questions as to how the work should be handled.

It also saves a great deal of time and postage to use an inker who lives nearby, with the additional advantage of not risking losing any pages in transit through the mail (insure your packages and get a signed receipt).

Another approach for those using inkers at a distance is to scan the pages, save them as JPEGs, and e-mail or transfer them via the Internet. The inker can then either print them out on Bristol board, use vellum over the printed-out page, or use a digital inking technique in which she inks right on the digital file (see Chapter 11).

It is a very good idea to get into the habit of scanning or photocopying the pencils as soon as they are finished, particularly if you're sending them out to be inked.

Lettering and Sound Effects

If you are doing conventional hand lettering, your penciled pages will be passed to the letterer before going to the inker. But if you are doing your own digital lettering, as most people do these days, you'll first scan the pencils and, using Photoshop or Illustrator's type tool, place the type in position on a separate layer of your image file. When you are happy with the type placement, the layers can be compressed and the page file sent on to the inker digitally. See Chapter 10 for a much more in-depth look at the lettering process. There is a good tutorial at ***www.balloontales.com/tips/balloon/index.html***, and ***http://hans.presto.tripod.com/links005.html*** has an index to lettering sites online.

Next, print out the lettered pages, cut out the balloons, and paste them directly onto the original art or on an acetate overlay. At this stage remember to save a copy of the file with the layers uncompressed; this enables easier type editing if changes are needed later.

Another option is outsourcing. If you are sending the file out to be lettered digitally or manually by someone else, you can scan the original page yourself or send the page for the letterer to scan herself and work from. No matter which option you choose, be sure to save a copy of the pencils for your own files.

If you are doing your own lettering, you will also have to handle sound effects. You may have to buy clip art bursts or use old comics for inspiration in creating the display lettering you need for your book. The penciler and writer have already agreed upon where they will be the most effective, now the decision must be made as to who will do sound effects and bursts. Traditionally this has been the letterer's job. If you are doing it yourself, this job will fall on your shoulders unless your inker has some expertise in this area and has agreed that he will do it.

The order in which you do the production on the project will depend on the choices you make at your planning meeting. When you have carefully considered your options as to who is doing what, you will be able to anticipate much better what your costs and production time will be.

E-QUESTION

WHY DO INDEPENDENT COMICS COST MORE THAN MARVEL AND DC BOOKS?

DC AND MARVEL HAVE LARGE PRINT RUNS THAT REQUIRE OFFSET PRINTING, AND THE MORE COPIES THAT ARE PRINTED THE LESS THE PER-UNIT COST. INDEPENDENT PUBLISHERS, WITH THEIR SMALLER PRINT RUNS, MUST CHARGE A HIGHER COVER PRICE AS A CONSEQUENCE.

Scanning to Coloring

Coloring is usually the final stage of the production process. Even if all the previous steps have been done the old-fashioned way, it is still possible at this point to enter the digital age and scan the line art for coloring. If you do so, a 600 dpi scan of the art is made and the colorist proceeds to do her job in one of the many painting programs available to artists today. If you have opted to hand color the art, this process is completed in much the same way as the previous ones: Art is fed in batches to the colorist, and production at all stages continues until the color artist has finished the entire book.

After the book is completed, the pages should be scanned, if they have not been already, and saved to a DVD or CDs. The partners on the project should all review the book, checking carefully for errors or technical problems. This is the (almost) last chance to make corrections before the book goes to press. You can make changes later on the proof from the printer, but the printer won't be happy and it won't be cheap.

Lastly, consult your printer as to their technical requirements and make arrangements to deliver the colored pages, cover art, and a *folding dummy* to them. A folding dummy is a mockup of the book that tells them what goes where. In preparing digital files, the printer's requirements for prepress are also really important.

A consultation with the printer's rep to double-check all technical specs is a good idea. Most printers have Web sites that will spell these requirements out quite clearly, but should you have any questions, a call to them should answer or resolve any doubts. Important questions you should ask are:

- Has the cost quoted to you changed?
- What are the payment terms?
- How should the files be saved?
- Will they be generating the color separations or will you?
- How long will the process of getting a proof to you take?
- Is the cost of the proof also included in the quote?
- Do they send you an actual color proof or blueline?
- Do they send a digital proof?
- How long after you have approved the proof will it take until the book is shipped?
- Do they have a facility where books can be stored and shipped as needed, or must you take delivery of the whole print run? (If you are using a POD publisher, storage will not be an issue.)

The person initially in charge of getting the print quote should be the print contact person for the project. Ideally, this person should have familiarity with printing; if not, they should familiarize themselves with printing terms and ask for clarification if anything is unclear.

COVER DESIGN

The cover is the first thing the world will notice about your project. Therefore, it must be as slick, eye-catching, and professional looking as possible with all the artistic and text elements in place and working together. In this chapter you'll learn about the various elements that go into making a cover design look eye-catching, intriguing, and professional. This chapter also discusses logo designs and production timing and methodology in relation to cover art.

Logo and Titles

The top of the page should be designed to leave what is referred to as *negative space* in printing. In other words, negative space is an area with little going on in it, deliberately designed to leave a place for the title and logo to appear at the top. The top left corner of the cover space is reserved for the company logo, although there seems to be a growing trend toward placing it on the back cover, perhaps to leave the front as uncluttered as possible.

A great deal of care and consideration should go into the design of your company's insignia and the book's title logo. If your first graphic novel is a huge hit, you will undoubtedly go on to publish other titles, so your logo should be emblematic of your company's personality and goals.

Death Hawk © 2006 Mark Ellis, art by Darryl Banks.

▲ Artist Darryl Banks designed this cover with plenty of negative space reserved, which enabled the designer to come up with a logo that didn't clash with or fight for attention with the rest of the cover design.

Formerly, graphic artists and art agencies did a lot of this sort of design, but with the advent of sophisticated graphic software, such as Photoshop, Illustrator, PageMaker, and Quark, logo design came within the reach of almost everyone with a little artistic flair and knowledge of the programs. When designing your own logo, be sure to save your designs as high-resolution files with at least 600 dpi.

Your company's logo will appear on the cover of the graphic novel and also at the top of press releases, agreements, and forms. The logo for the book cover usually is an abbreviated version of the main logo, with design elements singled out and boxed.

The book logo must stretch across the width of the cover and be striking and legible enough to immediately convey a clear visual impression. This is not the place for weird, quirky, or illegible fonts that will annoy rather than intrigue the reader.

Adobe Illustrator, Quark, and Freehand programs all have features that allow you to distort, stretch, and manipulate type in many ways into distinctive shapes and colors. It is not as easy to do this in PhotoShop, but it can be done, particularly in the later versions with better type tools.

E-FACT

JOE SHUSTER, CO-CREATOR OF *SUPERMAN*, DESIGNED THE UPWARD CURVING SUPERMAN LOGO. HE WAS INFLUENCED BY THE ART DECO VOGUE POPULAR IN THE 1930S. THE LOGO APPEARED EVEN IN THE EARLIEST PENCIL VERSIONS OF THE CHARACTER, AND ITS BASIC ELEMENTS HAVE REMAINED ESSENTIALLY UNCHANGED FOR SEVENTY YEARS.

Death Hawk © 2006 Mark Ellis, art by Melissa Martin Ellis.

Many comic logos use a 3-D effect with drop shadows and seem to recede into the distance toward the right of the page. They are often boldly colored and may contain a graphic element that ties into the theme of the book. Think *Green Arrow* or *Green Lantern*.

The *Superman* logo is iconic, as is that of *Batman*. They are so associated with the characters that you can't think of one without thinking of the other. If you are not sure of a design direction for the book logo, take a trip to your local comics store or bookstore to look at what is currently going on in the market.

▶ An early conception of the Superman character.

Superman © DC Comics.

Your goal is to be as distinctive as possible, without creating something that is not in harmony with the current trends of design and publishing.

If you are in doubt about a design but hope that by its strangeness it will stand out, rethink it. Graphic novel publishing is risky enough without taking a misstep on cover design.

◀ In this cover from *Death Hawk: The Soulworm Saga*, the title logo was designed to complement the colors used in the cover art. (See color insert for full-color art.)

Death Hawk © 2006 Mark Ellis. Art by Darryl Banks, colors by Melissa Martin Ellis.

Another element of the title logo design is careful color coordination with the palette of the cover art. Even if the logo looks good it could clash with the art. This presents a jarring, unprofessional appearance and could put off potential readers, and that may cost you sales.

Your company's logo will appear in two formats: the small boxed logo on book covers and the full-sized logo that goes on all your printed materials. The company logo should be done as early as possible in the timeline. As soon as you have done research on cost and other feasibility issues and decided to proceed with the project, a company logo should be designed. When designing a logo, try to create a one-of-a-kind look, something unique and distinctive. When your logo designs for the company and book logos are done well ahead of the completion date for the book, the images will be available for use in flyers, ads, and other promotional materials.

Not only will the logo make press releases, ads, and letters to distributors, vendors, contributors, and prospective suppliers look more professional, it will also give your creative team a real boost and sense of pride. If you are putting up a promotional Web site, a memorable logo is a must. Often just a logo can convey the idea that your graphic novel team is a publishing company and a profitable concern.

Since your cover price will be part of the cover, you will have to run a project cost analysis beforehand to make sure that your price adequately covers your printing and production expenses. The cover price is generally located on the back cover of graphic novels, right above the barcode and ISBN number. For more on ISBNs and barcodes, see Chapter 19.

Cover Art

Although a color cover says you're serious and possibly makes you more competitive in the marketplace than books with black-and-white covers, there are exceptions to the rules. *Michael Chabon Presents: The Amazing Adventures of the Escapist, Volume 1,* certainly proves this point. The two-color cover uses only black and red ink on white paper, but the design is so well planned and executed that it is attention grabbing as any four-color cover.

▶ This boxed logo from Millennium Publications had only the letter *M*, an element from the hand–lettered full logo design.

Millennium logo © Melissa Martin.

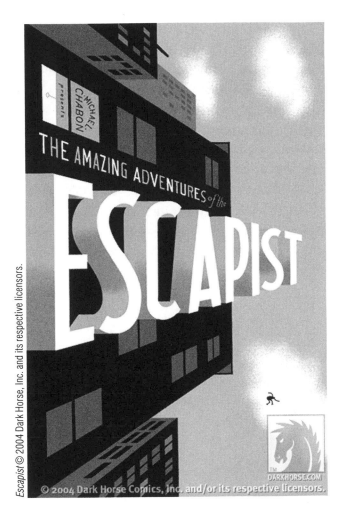

Escapist © 2004 Dark Horse, Inc. and its respective licensors.

◀ This two-color cover is so well designed it is just as eye-catching as a four-color one.

The designer used a clever forced-perspective effect and gray screens to give the image a surprising richness. In most instances, however, color is more expensive than black and white, but it is usually worth the cost. This is not the component of the novel on which to attempt to cut costs.

When you are in the initial stages of the project, or at the first planning meeting, discuss ideas for the cover with your partner(s). At least three approaches or concepts should be considered, and the cover artist, who is more than likely your penciler, should have a lot of input as to the direction the art will take.

Obviously, the lead characters should be on the cover doing something action oriented, interesting, or intriguing. It should also be apparent what genre the novel is, be it superhero, action adventure, or whatever category it falls into.

Some graphic novels veer away from this approach, opting for a minimalistic design more similar to regular book covers with the page divided into graphic areas distinguished mainly by color and graphic elements taking a backseat to the overall design scheme.

This approach requires good design control and is difficult, although when it is done well it conveys a more sophisticated, upscale look.

Pantheon Books' *Darwin for Beginners*, *Freud for Beginners*, *Einstein for Beginners*, and *Marx for Beginners* are good examples of a simple design approach that works well. Single-color backgrounds, a large graphical depiction of the book's subject rendered as a caricature, and the subject names in large type with "For Beginners" below in small type are design elements carried throughout the series. Uncomplicated and intriguing, the simplicity draws the eye.

Balancing elements can be a challenge, but ideally the cover is eye-catching but not chaotic, colorful but not garish, and sufficiently interesting that even a casual reader will want to pick up the book and flip through it.

The cover is not the place to feature graphic violence or sexual situations unless you are looking to fill a niche market. This doesn't mean you shouldn't feature scantily clad females, since they seem to be a publishing staple, but some restraint should be exercised if your goal is to get large bookstore chains to carry the book.

© 2003 by Pantheon Books, a division of Random House.

▲ *Darwin for Beginners*, by Jonathan Miller and Borin Van Loon; *Einstein For Beginners* by Joseph Schwartz and Michael McGuinness.

As far as production goes, early on you must decide whether the cover artist will also ink and color the page or whether the services of other artists will be used for those aspects of it. This is a personal decision and really depends on whether the penciler feels comfortable with inking and coloring. A painted cover usually conveys good production values and may help to sell the book, so if possible, either through a real painting or through a digital painting, this approach is a good idea. If it isn't possible, just be sure the color artist produces a great interpretation of the art in her work. If the painting or coloring is done digitally, it will be possible to try different approaches and color schemes by saving different versions of the files. This can be a hugely helpful design tool.

E-FACT

IN THE 1990S, WRAPAROUND COVERS WERE USED FOR DIFFERENT COMIC TITLES THAT WERE TIED IN WITH ONE ANOTHER TO ENTICE THE READER TO BUY ALL THE DIFFERENT ISSUES AND FIT THEM TOGETHER LIKE THE PIECES OF A PUZZLE TO FORM ONE LARGE IMAGE.

Often a well-known artist in the graphic narrative field is commissioned to produce the cover, which not only ensures a professional appearance, but the cover can be used as a promotional tool to draw in readers who are fans of that particular artist's work. This can be an expensive proposition, so think it through very carefully before reaching a decision.

Wraparound Covers

What is a wraparound cover? The term itself is self-explanatory—it is simply a cover design that spills over or continues onto the back cover, carrying the same artistic elements. Visionary Jim Steranko is generally credited with creating the wraparound as it applies to comics, using the form for his two-volume *Steranko History of Comics*. However, it is a relatively recent development in the comics field. It didn't come into common usage until the late 1980s and then was used mainly as a marketing and promotional tool.

As long as you have a concept in mind for the cover, it is really not that much more difficult to design a wraparound cover for the book. Bear in mind that perfect-bound books will have a spine, and the thickness of it will vary based on the page count of your novel and even the type of paper.

This is a technical issue that should be thoroughly discussed with your printer. You will also need to know about proper sizing of the image and bleed areas. This is one reason you should get quotes and line up potential printers early in the project's timeline.

Wild, Wild West © 2006 Paramount Pictures.

▲ This beautifully designed and rendered wraparound cover for the first issue of *The Wild, Wild West* comic book from Millennium Publications was painted by Adam Hughes.

Take into account the fact that the design of the wraparound cover will be interrupted by the book's spine, but as long as you're aware of that, it should pose no problem. The wraparound cover gives the cover artist an extra opportunity to shine, plus it gets more information to readers before they even open the book.

The back cover can be all art or graphic elements, or it may contain text, a brief synopsis of the book, or possibly the credits. Since you are already paying for color printing here, you might as well make full use of it and design a cover that will knock their socks off!

CHAPTER 15

PRINT PRODUCTION

Unless you plan to market your product exclusively as an online e-zine, it is important that you understand the different technical aspects of print production. There are many elements that require your attention in order to ensure that your project, in which you have invested so much time, effort, and money, comes out looking the way you had hoped it would. Knowing the printing process will also help you to communicate clearly with your printer, which is vitally important to the overall process.

Understanding the Printing Process

There are two kinds of offset printing technologies: web and sheet-fed. Web presses produce large print runs on giant rolls of paper. They were the primary means of printing comics during the golden and silver ages of the medium. The main advantages of using web presses are speed and cost. Web presses are cost-effective when you require a print run in excess of ten thousand units. The disadvantages are poorer paper quality and sometimes poorer overall quality control and color registration. Most independent publishers don't have orders in sufficient numbers to use web press printers.

▲ ▶ Print technology, which began in the fifteenth century when Gutenberg invented the printing press, changed the world.

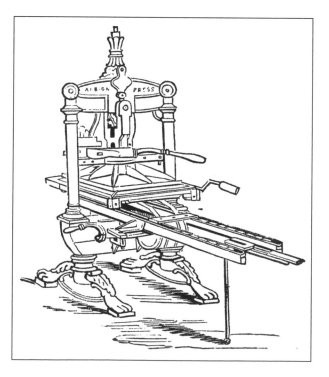

Sheet-fed presses handle smaller jobs and are used by customers requiring shorter print runs and higher quality color control and registration. Digital presses, both color and black and white, are used in today's quick turnaround print-on-demand, or POD, market.

Your understanding of what is needed by the printer in any of these processes will be required to make the best choice when picking your print service provider. The printer will need the following information from you:

- Number of copies needed
- Number of pages, not including the cover
- Color of inside pages: single color, two colors, or four colors
- Color on the covers, including inside front and inside back: single color, two color, or four color

You can ask what the cost difference is between these options and get a quote with the different options noted.

▲ Web presses are enormous and can fill entire rooms. They have to be to accommodate the huge rolls of paper used in web printing.

▲ Small sheet-fed presses such as this A. B. Dick have been used in the printing industry for decades.

PANTONE COLOR CHART

▶ Pantone color charts have ink colors in all their many permutations, plus a reference number that exactly identifies each color.

You should also ask prospective printers some questions:

- Can you do perfect-bound soft covers?
- Are digital files acceptable or do you require the original artwork be shipped to you?
- If you accept digital files, what software and format are required?
- What is your policy on proofs? Are there extra charges for them?
- What is your payment policy?
- How long after I approve a proof will the job be ready?
- What options do you offer on paper and cover stock? Can you send samples?
- What size options are available?
- Are organic inks and recycled papers available?
- Do you guarantee your work?

If you're printing in color, you will definitely need to see a color proof, even if there is an extra charge involved. If you opt out of this choice, be prepared for unpleasant surprises.

A quick reference guide to printing terms in plain English can be found at the PrintUSA Web site: **www.printusa.com/glos.htm**.

Printers and Estimates

Sooner rather than later is a good time to start shopping around for the company that will print your book. Look for ads in trade journals such as the *Comic Buyer's Guide* to help locate prospective printers. There are now printers who cater to the niche market of comics and graphic novels. Contacting them is a good place to start getting organized and to get a sense of what will be required on your end.

Not too long ago the process of offset printing a four-color publication often involved a process so complicated that it was filled with opportunities for glitches, errors, and snafus. Multiple film negatives of every page were shot to represent the colors cyan, magenta, yellow, and black, or CMYK in printing parlance.

- **Black** = 0% brightness, 100% grey.
- **White** = 100% brightness, 0% grey.
- **Grey** is most often specified from white = 0, thus 10% grey = 90% brightness.

◀ A standard grayscale will give you an idea of the percentage of ink coverage from zero to 100 percent.

Numerous things could and did happen to mess up the process—negatives assembled in the wrong order or shot at the wrong screen percentage could really impact the results in amazingly bad ways.

Even today's streamlined digital process is fraught with the potential for errors. Even those with a printing background and years of knowledge are often faced with situations where printers, pushed for time and using procedures over which they did not exercise proper quality control, try to pass off inferior work as good enough for a comic book.

So for those heading into the turbulent world of printing, choose a printer who comes highly recommended, who has printed product similar to yours, and who is willing to show you samples of their work and to supply references. Be wary of choosing the lowest bidder if he has no references and no samples or tries to rush you into committing. Reputable printers will work with you and not apply pressure.

Your project is too important to entrust to someone without the proper expertise. It represents hundreds of hours of work and thousands of dollars, so don't trip up over a matter of pennies when you're so near the finish line.

Only after you have gathered the necessary information and costs can you really begin to plan the production flow for the book.

Information you learn from the printer at the initial stages of the project will impact other decisions you make further down the line, so waste no time in contacting prospective print suppliers. Your call or e-mail should simply ask for a print quote, using the parameters previously listed. The printer has representatives that do nothing all day but figure these quotes; they are happy to do so and you should not feel any hesitancy about getting the figures even though your project is in its early stages.

Page Proofs and Color Separators

As technology keeps changing, more and more production processes are being done digitally. Traditionally, the process of separating color for printing involved first photographing the artwork three times using a filter for each color. This produces three grayscale images, which represent the red, green, and blue components of the original. When negatives of these images are shot, the resulting images produce the cyan, magenta, and yellow separation negatives used to burn printing plates. A fourth black plate is shot to provide the crispness and contrast in shadow areas, and you now have the components necessary to make a reasonable approximation of the original.

As anyone can readily see, this process is tricky, and human error enters into the equation at numerous places in the process, particularly when each color must be screened and imposed at a slightly different angle as it is burned into a printing plate.

The screened image, called a halftone, is composed of tiny dots that when superimposed over the other colors produce a blended effect, which ideally should closely resemble the original. If even one of the color plates isn't burned correctly, the result is an image where the dots don't line up correctly. This is what is meant by an image being *out of register*.

The size of the dot produced and how much it spreads on the page is very much influenced by the absorbency of the type of paper used. This is called *dot gain*, and it must be taken into account when preparing the image for the printer.

Digital technology in the past few decades has changed the face of the industry, giving rise to better control of the processes of color separating and printing. Stochastic screening, a process whereby dots of the same size are randomly placed, eliminates moiré effects like those occasionally generated by traditional halftones. In addition, digital printers sometimes add two extra colors to the process to produce an image with much greater depth and similarity to the original.

Perhaps the most striking improvement in the technology is the computer-to-plate (CTP) technology, which has allowed printers to eliminate the film part of the procedure entirely. In the CTP process, the images and dots are burned directly onto the printing plate with a laser. It increases quality, saves money, and is environmentally friendly.

As you search for a printer that will fill your needs, you will need to find out who offers you page proofs and, in the case of four-color work, chromalins, matchprints, or color keys.

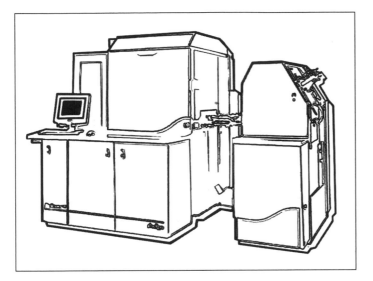

 An Indigo digital printer represents the latest advance in print technology, which will undoubtedly keep improving.

It is now possible for desktop publishers to generate their own color separations, but it would be wise to talk to your printer about the feasibility of doing this. Some money can be saved, but it is a highly technical process that may better be left in the hands of trained professionals.

E-FACT

BEN FRANKLIN STARTED OUT AS A PRINTER AND CONSIDERED IT A NOBLE PROFESSION. NO MATTER HOW FAMOUS HE BECAME AS A WRITER AND A STATESMAN, THAT IS HOW HE ALWAYS IDENTIFIED HIMSELF, EVEN IN HIS LAST WILL AND TESTAMENT, WHICH BEGINS "I, BENJAMIN FRANKLIN OF PHILADELPHIA, PRINTER. . . . "

If you are producing your book the old-fashioned way, scanned from your original pages, you will need to work with a color separator. A good approach is to first find your printer, and then ask them for recommendations as to a separator. Printers and separators who have worked together have good communication skills and can tailor their specifications to each other's equipment more easily. If this is not an option, ask the printer what kind of sep they need for their color profile.

After this brief description of the color separation process, it should be abundantly clear why, if you're printing your book in color, you need to see a color proof even if there is an extra charge involved.

Print on Demand

Oh brave new world that has such people in it! In a world where printing may be one of the most complicated and confusing things you'll ever encounter short of rocket science, enter digital printing and print on demand (POD).

POD is made possible by the new digital technology and may well be the future of printing. It certainly offers the small publisher options that were not available only a few years ago. It gives hope to writers and artists who found themselves stymied by the cost and constraints of regular printing and publishing. Still, careful screening and review of references is highly recommended for those choosing a service provider in this relatively new industry.

Here is a short list of the advantages and drawbacks inherent in this type of printing.

Advantages:
1. It allows a complete book to be printed and bound in a few hours.
2. It is designed for short print runs.
3. Books need not be printed until they are ordered.
4. Books need not be stored.
5. Books can be offered on company Web sites and made available as downloadable PDF files.

Disadvantages:
1. Some POD publishers try to control your book, demanding royalties and retaining rights.
2. Poor quality control.
3. High per-unit cost.

What should you look for in a POD service provider? First, run, don't walk, away from POD providers that try to claim copyrights to your intellectual property. The creators should not sign any document or an online agreement that contains language that could be interpreted as an assignation of any rights to the POD provider.

E-QUESTION

WHAT IS THE DIFFERENCE BETWEEN PRINT ON DEMAND (POD) AND SELF-PUBLISHING?

IN SELF-PUBLISHING, THE AUTHOR RETAINS CONTROL OF ALL ASPECTS OF THE PROCESS AND ALL RIGHTS. HE ALSO KEEPS ALL REVENUES FROM SALES. IN POD PUBLISHING, THE AUTHORS' CHOICES CAN BE LIMITED AS TO FORMAT, DESIGN, AND OTHER ASPECTS OF THE BOOK'S APPEARANCE, PLUS SOME OF THE REVENUES AND RIGHTS TO THEIR PROPERTY ARE CONTROLLED BY THE POD PUBLISHER.

Although some printers and even publishers might try to get away with this trickery, keep in mind that to assign or convey any kind of rights to your intellectual property to another party a separate agreement that spells everything out specifically must be signed by all parties. Also, you should be able to set the cover price and control all aspects of the publishing process, including keeping all proceeds from the sale of your product.

There are some publishers out there that prey on innocent creators. You need to thoroughly review all policies and ask questions if there are any aspects of the arrangement that you don't understand. Costs can be substantially increased by charges not included in the initial package, such as renewal fees, extra charges for obtaining an ISBN number or copyright registration, and ambiguous legal fees. When you're assessing a service and comparing quotes, be sure to check for these costs.

Having said that, the number of POD printers are growing every day and there are plenty out there who offer basic, straightforward services with no strings attached.

E-SSENTIAL

IMAGE AREA IS THE TERM PRINTERS USE FOR THE AREA WHERE INK WILL PRINT ON A PAGE. BLEED IS THE TERM USED FOR AN IMAGE OR INK COVERAGE THAT EXTENDS BEYOND THE USUAL PAGE AREA SO THAT WHEN IT IS TRIMMED IT RUNS RIGHT OFF THE PAGE. THE GRIPPER AREA CONTAINS NO IMAGE BECAUSE THE PAGE EDGE IS GRASPED TO PULL IT THROUGH THE PRESS AT THIS POINT.

Self-promotion and distribution issues also arise when using POD providers. Books from companies that offer POD are usually available through the companies' Web sites and from Amazon.com and other online booksellers. Many POD providers also list books in the catalogs of major wholesalers, such as Ingram.

Although this theoretically means they will be available for order at bookstores, in actuality the POD provider's policies may effectively block sales.

Bookstores are accustomed to receiving a 40 percent or more discount, up to ninety days in a billing cycle, plus returnability of unsold copies. A POD provider that doesn't work within those parameters may never sell much product to bookstore chains, known in the trade as brick-and-mortar stores.

However, if you are aware of the pitfalls and shortcomings of print on demand, you may find a company that will meet your needs at a reasonable cost and offer you an opportunity to get your book into the marketplace when other options fail.

Research on the Internet the printers that have built up a clientele in the comics and graphic novel field. Some companies have instant quote forms on their Web sites and you can gather information about costs and services.

Here's a list of printers to get you started:

- Ka-blam, Florida:
  www.ka-blam.com

- All Ages Comic Book Publishers:
  www.icomics.com

- Udo Printing/SIPS comics:
  www.udoprinting.com

- CMYK Graphix Inc.:
  www.cmykgraphix.com

- Overseas Printing Corporation:
  www.overseasprinting.com

- PrintMedia Books.com:
  www.printmediabooks.com

- Whitehall Printing:
  www.whitehallprinting.com

- King Printing:
  www.kingprinting.com

- Star Print Brokers:
  www.starprintbrokers.com

- Town & Country Reprographics:
  www.reprographic.com
  Both offset and POD.

- Publishers' Graphics:
  www.pubgraphics.com/short_run_book_print.html
  A short-run printer; their Web site asserts they are very quality conscious.

- Brenner Printing:
  www.brennerprinting.com/comic/index.htm
  They have been in business for many years and are currently transitioning to going totally digital prepress.

- Fidlar Doubleday, Inc.:
  http://fidlardoubleday.com/pages/dpw.html
  Digital printers; they have downloadable quote request forms on their Web site.

- Lightning Source:
  www.lightningsource.com/index.htm
  POD printers, e-book distributors, and distribution to distributors.

- Stickman Graphics' Web site has a comprehensive list of printers
  www.stickmangraphics.com/resourceD.htm

CHAPTER 16

STORAGE AND SHIPPING

After your many months of hard work and planning, the happy day will eventually arrive when your books are printed and you hold them in your hands for the first time. Then a realization will dawn and a question will occur to you: "Where will I store my first shipment of books? What arrangements will I need to make as far as storage goes, either at a facility I control or at the printer's warehouse?"

Printer's Storage and Shipping

In the early stages of planning production for your project, you called and received quotes from many potential print service providers. In the midst of all the technical talk and price and service comparison shopping you had better remember to ask about storage and shipping. If you didn't check out the arrangement and options available to you, then the entire shipment will arrive at your home or at a mini-storage facility. Having handled the reception of hundreds of boxes of books ourselves in the past, plus their subsequent distribution, we can tell you that this is not a chore for the faint-hearted.

You should inquire as to the cost of the printer storing your books and handling the shipping to the distribution points. If a printer offers an array of services and her print quote is very low, it may be very tempting to use her, despite the fact that she cannot handle storing and shipping the product. Weighing all the factors involved in the decision is a process you and your partners will have to consider carefully. Some of the issues you must consider are:

- How much cheaper is the print quote from the next highest bidder who *does* offer shipping and storage?
- How many books are you having printed? Is it at all feasible to store and ship the books from your own location?
- If so, who will handle taking delivery of the boxes, stacking and storing them, and be responsible for order fulfillment?

- Will the same person handle the management of orders, printing the labels, and manage the shipping forms and records?
- Did the printer offer a shipping cost estimate and state if they use a system whereby they report what they have shipped and when it went out?

Most printers who offer book storage will provide it at no cost or at a small charge. They also will have a system in place whereby they can track orders and provide you with detailed shipping information, more than likely through an online Web link to the company's Web site.

E-FACT

USING A PRINTER WHO CAN SHIP OUT YOUR BOOKS FOR YOU IS AN ENORMOUS SAVINGS OF BOTH TIME AND ENERGY. HANDLING YOUR OWN SHIPPING AND STORAGE AND THE ASSOCIATED RECORD KEEPING CAN BE A TIME-CONSUMING PROCESS THAT IS BETTER LEFT TO THE PROFESSIONALS.

If a printer hesitates when you inquire about the details of their shipping procedures, it may indicate that they do not have a good system in place. To have peace of mind, you must be able to know where your books are at all times and be able to send a response to customers who inquire where their product is or when they can expect delivery. If your printer is handling this but cannot communicate the information to you, it makes you look less professional in the eyes of your customers. This may well impact the sale of future books.

If you opt to use a POD service, you can eliminate two headaches as most POD providers handle shipping and storage as well as printing. If you choose this option, be very clear as to what their shipping policies are. Questions you should ask are:

- How will my books be shipped?
- What are the costs involved?
- How can I track my books?
- If books are lost or damaged in shipping, who is responsible and who will bear the replacement costs and handle the paperwork involved in getting the situation straightened out?

If you are having only a small quantity of books printed, you will almost certainly end up using the POD production method. If this is the case, you will have streamlined the process to a great extent, but be sure to do your homework. Get the answers beforehand to reduce stress and anxiety later, and get all your questions answered in writing if possible.

Storage Tips for Art and Books

You may not even have considered it before, but the storage of art used to create your graphic novel can become an issue. If you use old-fashioned production methods you will have over a hundred pages of original art, the penciled and inked pages, and possibly the colored pages as well.

Why take such care of the art once the book has been printed? Any number of reasons come to mind, not the least of which is the fact that you put so much effort and money into the creation of this art. In addition, it is original art and as such it is irreplaceable. Digital files can be lost or become corrupted and negatives can be destroyed, but if the originals exist, the files can always be replaced.

If you have prepared promotional and advertising materials, you will add some additional pages to the total with flyers, proofs, brochures, and industry ads. Granted, some of these items can be disregarded if you have used computer coloring or have prepared your ads as digital files. But even if the latter is the case, you probably created promo art for the ads and flyers that will require storage.

Original art should always be stored in acid-free packaging. If you use cardboard or paper containers, be sure they are marked acid-free. Preferable to these are the plastic storage bins widely available with airtight lids. These have numerous advantages, not the least of which is the fact that they are better at keeping air and moisture away from the art. Many people used to cover each individual page with a sheet of tissue paper, but this is not strictly necessary. If this method is used, again, be sure the paper and tape is acid free or you can cause more problems than you solve by their use.

Moisture and mold are the biggest enemies of paper over time, so keep the lids on the bins and store them in an area without big temperature fluctuations (not the basement or attic). Stacking bins can hold a lot of material in a small amount of space.

E-SSENTIAL

BASEMENTS MAY BE HANDY AND CONVENIENT, BUT EVEN IF IT HAS NEVER FLOODED BEFORE AND HAS A DEHUMIDIFIER, NEVER STORE ORIGINAL ART OR BOOKS THAT YOU WOULD LIKE TO KEEP MOLD-FREE IN THE BASEMENT. HOWEVER, IF ITEMS ARE PLACED IN PLASTIC STORAGE BINS ON SHELVES THAT ARE SEVERAL FEET OFF THE FLOOR, YOU MAY BE IN SAFE TERRITORY.

Old-fashioned filing cabinets never really go out of style. Your office should contain at least one filing cabinet, perhaps more, to hold copies or scans of art, ads, flyers, posters, and their supporting artwork.

Computer files are just as subject to damage as files in the real world, so always have backups. A good system consists of having two versions of all digital files, one backed up on removable media and one on the computer, and lastly a hard-copy version stored in your filing cabinet. This triple redundancy system should insure your files for the appreciation of future generations.

Remember: Even if your pages yellow over time or have faded or developed splotches and stains, they can be scanned and copies restored to good condition despite what might at first glance seem like unfixable damage. Today's technology offers hope for art that might have been thrown away just a few short years ago (*see examples on following pages*).

The important thing to remember about artwork storage is to file as you go. Pages can become damaged and dog-eared if you wait until the entire book is done to begin thinking about proper storage. It isn't the most glamorous job in the world and most artists aren't known for their meticulousness, but remind yourself that your art is important and deserves respect.

Shipping Strategies

If you have decided not to use a POD service provider or printer who handles your storage and shipping, you will find yourself in the unenviable position of handling the shipping chores yourself. That's the bad news. The good news is . . . well, unfortunately, there really isn't any. You will have to get organized and work out a storage location and a system to handle labeling, shipping, and tracking. That's okay, since by this point you have probably honed your organizational skills to a high degree of efficiency.

Your storage space need not be expensive or elaborate, but it should be fairly close to where your shipping area is to avoid a lot of exertion. It should also be in a dry and temperature-controlled space. The tape used to seal cardboard boxes can become loose over time due to heat and humidity. If it gives way during shipping, you are in trouble. Also, storing boxes in an area where moisture is a factor can expose the materials to insects.

The best place to store the boxes may be an unused corner of your shipping area, provided there is enough space. You'll need a scale and your computer close by, too.

Setting up an account with a shipping service will require a few phone calls or visits to the Internet. Three factors to consider for the best deal are cost, speed, and reliability.

The shippers you might consider using are:

- United Parcel Service (UPS):
  www.ups.com (main Web page)
  www.ups.com/content/us/en/welcome/index.html (page for new customers)
- The United States Postal Service (USPS):
  www.usps.com (main Web page)
  www.usps.com/business/shippingtools/welcome.htm (for business packages)
- Federal Express (FedEx):
  www.fedex.com (main Web page)
  www.fedex.com/us/newcustomer/index.html?link=4 (for new customers)
- DHL:
  www.dhl-usa.com/home/home.asp (main Web page)

New technological advances allow you to print out shipping labels and postage from your own computer plus schedule a pickup. UPS has an elaborate online system in place that allows you to figure out your options in regard to destination, time, costs, pickup or dropoff, and package size for your shipment. With this feature you can change the variables to see how it affects the cost quite easily.

The USPS site also has pages that allow you to calculate postage and a page that talks about ground shipping: *www.usps.com/all/shippingand mailing/groundpackages.htm.*

The USPS is now working with UPS, so a careful comparison of their prices is in order.

The FedEx and DHL sites require you to register and log in before they will provide a detailed quote.

The USPS offers a lot of mailing options, including Priority, First Class, Parcel Post, and Media Mail. First Class Mail is the cheapest for items such as envelopes and small boxes, while Parcel Post or Media Mail are least expensive for heavy packages. Parcel Post is usually cheaper than UPS, and where there is no rush and time is definitely not a factor, the USPS Media Mail option is a good value for consumers shipping books. Packages cannot weigh in at more than fifteen pounds and they may take up to two weeks to arrive at their destination, so review the requirements carefully.

▲ An example of a badly damaged page that has already been scanned (*left*) and needs to be repaired in Photoshop (*right*).

The Miskatonic Project © 2006 Mark Ellis, pencils by Don Heck, inks by Robert Lewis.

It is hard to compare options, but some say the biggest advantages of USPS Priority Mail are the free boxes and faster shipping speeds, which are often faster than UPS, although not necessarily cheaper. USPS lightweight packages are not much more expensive to ship using Priority Mail, especially if sent to nearby destinations, and may cost as little as a dime more than shipping it Parcel Post.

The United States Postal Service's disadvantages are that their insurance costs extra, except in the case of their rather expensive Express Mail, and the USPS online tracking system usually provides only the bare minimum of information.

For medium to heavy boxes, USPS's flat rate Priority Mail should be considered. Their boxes are free and you pay the same flat rate amount as long as the box's weight doesn't go over seventy pounds.

UPS's advantage is that it offers fast shipping and is often cheaper than Priority Mail, FedEx, and USPS Parcel Post, especially in the case of heavy packages. It is generally faster than Parcel Post or Media Mail but slower than DHL, Priority Mail, and FedEx. With UPS, insurance for valuables worth up to $100 is included free of additional charges. You can find a UPS store near you by going to the main UPS Web site and clicking on the Locations tab.

When time is the main concern, not saving money, FedEx works well. It is generally more expensive than USPS or DHL, but it is usually very fast and provides the most detailed online tracking system.

Whether to use DHL depends mainly upon the part of the country an item is shipping from and where it is going. DHL is often less expensive than FedEx and UPS and offers very fast delivery to some locations. Whether shipping is very fast or rather slow just seems to be a function of location. DHL provides online tracking at no additional cost, and the tracking system shows more detailed information than some of the other shippers. DHL only offers free boxes for their Air Express service.

CHAPTER 17

ADVERTISING

Advertising is as important to the success of your graphic novel as maintaining good production values and creating a compelling story. It is your means of communicating your enthusiasm for your work to the world at large, plus it is a way of making people sufficiently intrigued by what they see to buy it. In this chapter you'll read about the various ways you can get your message out to the marketplace and tips for increasing the allure of your product.

Ad and Flyer Design

Your two primary means of communicating in print are flyers and advertising. Both can be expensive and require careful planning and strategizing. If you are getting quotes from various printers, research their prices for flyer and poster printing while at their Web sites. Often the printers' Web sites, particularly the ones geared toward comics and graphic novels, will have ways of promoting your book through an online affiliate or online store. Don't underestimate the potential of reaching a wider audience through these options.

The actual designing of ads, flyers, and posters will probably fall on the shoulders of the penciler and inker, and if rendered in color, then the colorist will be involved as well. More than likely you will find the cost of four-color ads a bit prohibitive, but you still may choose to do a color flyer or poster.

The images you select to convey your advertising message are the key element of any promotional material. A strong, professionally executed central image is vital. It should feature key characters or dramatic action, preferably both. The images you choose must catch the readers' attention and make them say, "Wow, that looks interesting!"

Art by Don Hillsman.

⚠ An advertisement for a 1992 biographical comic featuring the life of Malcolm X.

All characters © 1994–2007 Mark Ellis. Artwork by Darryl Banks and Melissa Martin Ellis.

▲ A promotional poster created for a start-up comics company featuring the first three titles to be launched.

Give a great deal of consideration as to what these images will be since they must stand out from the crowd. The advertising art should be striking, well executed, and simple enough to be grasped in the few fleeting seconds you have to capture the reader's attention.

Ad copy should be kept to a minimum—make every word count. Don't forget to include information such as when the project will be released and contact information for those interested in ordering directly from you in your ads and flyers. The copy in posters should contain even less text, such as the name of the property and a catch phrase or your company name.

E-ALERT

IN THE WORLD OF ADVERTISING, THE HOOKS THAT SNARE READERS ARE USUALLY IMAGES FEATURING SEX, THE BIZARRE, HUMOR, OR EVEN A COMBINATION OF ALL THREE. IF POSSIBLE, CREATE AN IMAGE THAT HAS AT LEAST TWO OUT OF THREE! POSSIBLY SUCH AN IMAGE ALREADY EXISTS IN THE BOOK AND CAN BE ADAPTED TO THE AD.

Keep in mind that magazines and newspapers stick to strict schedules, so planning and reserving advertising space well ahead of time (often two months in advance) of sending in the ad copy is often necessary.

▶ An ad announcing the release of the first issue of H. P. Lovecraft's *Cthulhu*.

Art by Daryl Hutchinson, Darryl Banks, and Melissa Martin.

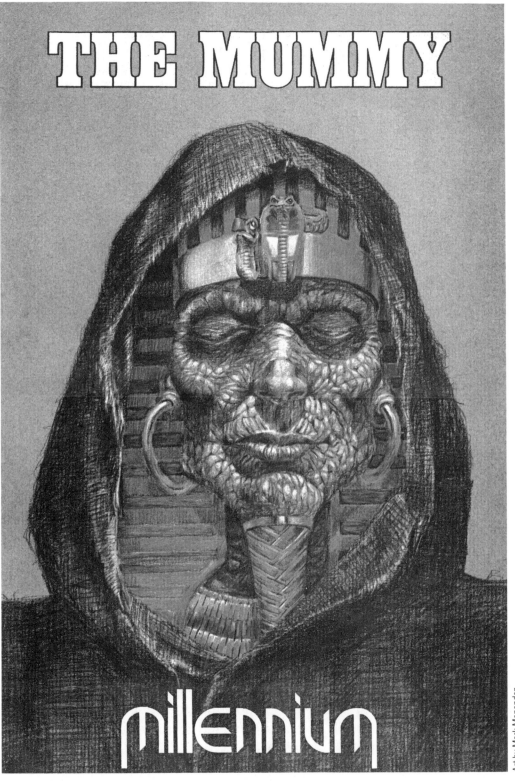

A very well-received promotional poster for the first issue of Anne Rice's *The Mummy*.

Art by Mark Menendez.

Ads that require no production at the publisher need to be *camera ready*, which means you need to do the ad layout yourself and provide high-res files or film or supply color separations if you're preparing a color ad. Some publications insist on only camera-ready materials, while some will perform the production for you. In our experience, you'll usually be happier with the design and production you do yourself in a program such as Quark, Photoshop, or PageMaker.

Flyers are promotional tools that, if executed properly, can be tremendously helpful in conveying your message to potential buyers. They provide you the opportunity to showcase the quality of the artwork and design plus tell a little bit about the storyline.

E-ALERT

FLYERS AND INSERTS CAN BE A VERY EFFECTIVE MEANS OF REACHING A MARKET THAT IS FLOODED WITH ADVERTISING PRODUCTS, BUT THE IMAGES YOU CHOOSE MUST BE SUFFICIENTLY PROFESSIONAL AND UNUSUAL TO HOLD THEIR OWN AGAINST THE BIG PUBLISHERS LIKE MARVEL AND DC AND ALL THE OTHER INDEPENDENT PUBLISHERS. SO PLAN WELL AND CHOOSE YOUR IMAGES CAREFULLY.

If done really well, you greatly increase the odds that people will be intrigued enough to check out your book. If the art is good and the actual text memorable, more than likely they'll keep it around for months or put it up on the wall as a poster, so you increase the likelihood of others seeing it as well.

Check out the cost of flyer and poster production when you are shopping for a printer. If your printer doesn't offer either of these services, there are plenty who do. Plus, it often pays to shop around for the best price. Flyers and posters are effective marketing tools and can be inserted in comics publications or mailed directly to potential customers and retailers.

Comics Publications

A comics-related publication that has been around since 1971 is the *Comics Buyer's Guide*, or *CBG*. This magazine-format periodical is read by both industry professionals and fans. It features four-color covers and black-and-white interiors, although there are also some color pages. Editor Maggie Thompson and contributors Tony Isabella and Peter David have been involved with the publication for a very long time. The *CBG* is almost required reading for those who are interested in the field of comics and graphic novels. At one time it was the *Variety* of the comic-book industry. It has reviews, articles, trivia, and lists of new comic-book and graphic novel releases.

Advertising rates vary. If you sign a contract to run ads multiple times, the discount increases as the number of insertions rise. Contracts can be for three, six, or twelve insertions, and, naturally, the more ads you place the cheaper they are per insertion, but you are also committed to a large outlay of cash for advertising costs.

1) Q: WHO INVENTED THE ROCKETPACK?

2) Q: WHO'S HIDEAWAY IS THE FORTRESS OF SOLITUDE?

3) Q: WHO KNOWS WHAT EVIL LURKS IN THE HEARTS OF MEN?

1) A: DOC SAVAGE
2) A: DOC SAVAGE
3) A: THE SHADOW*
*BUT THAT'S ANOTHER STORY...

DOC SAVAGE
THE MAN OF BRONZE

MILLENNIUM

BE THERE WHEN THE *REAL DOC* RETURNS!

COMING IN OCTOBER!

Art by Darryl Banks.

▲ A full-page ad that appeared in the *Comics Buyer's Guide* to launch the first issue of *Doc Savage: The Man of Bronze*.

A one-time insertion is called an open rate, and a quarter-page black-and-white ad can be placed for under $500, a half-page ad for under $800. The *CBG* offers a 15 percent discount for camera-ready copy. As well as display ads, it also offers marketplace ads, eBay/Showcase ads, a Comics Shop Directory, Web Directory, and Classified ads. The Web address is **www.cbgxtra.com**.

Comics & Games Retailer, a sister publication to the *CBG*, is geared toward retailers rather than the consumer market, although it does contain much information pertinent to publishers about industry statistics and trends. It also has regular industry columns by award-winning comics retailers, publishers, and professionals such as Ward Batty of Dr. No's, Joe Field of Flying Colors Comics, Chris Powell of Lone Star Comics, Phil Boyle of Coliseum of Comics, and Mimi Cruz-Carroll of Night Flight Comics.

Comics Price Guide.com (*www.comicsprice guide.com*) is an online site with both free and premium membership that offers information on what's hot and what's not, which may be helpful in tracking trends.

The *Comic Shop News* is a full-color, eight- to twelve-page free weekly newspaper distributed to six hundred comic book shops worldwide. Cliff Biggers and Ward Batty started it back in 1987, and both are still associated with the publication. The larger publishers comprise ninety percent of *CSN*'s ad sales, and please note they do not allow advertisers to put subscription offers, mail-order advertisements, or their company's addresses in their ads. Biggers and Batty say the reason for this restriction is because the purpose of *Comic Shop News* is to stimulate sales in the direct market. Each issue contains news, interviews, and a monthly checklist with Diamond order numbers and color art.

Wizard was founded in 1991 by Gareb Shamus, and their site (*www.wizarduniverse.com*) has a lot of information that may be of interest to comics professionals. Their Thursday Morning Quarterback section contains reviews by *Wizard* staffers of the week's new releases. This site is abuzz with industry news and reviews.

Wizard claims a circulation of 185,000 and a readership (94 percent male, median age twenty-five) of nearly 900,000. With ad rates that start around $2,300 for a black-and-white quarter-page ad and $7,500 to insert posters, you will need very deep pockets if you want to advertise in *Wizard*.

Diamond Comic Distributors and Other Catalogs

The largest direct-market distributor, Diamond Comic Distributors, publishes a catalog, *Previews*, that comes out once a month. It contains listings of new comic book and graphic novel projects scheduled to be released in the near future. Every month the printed version of the *Previews* catalog has around 3,500 individual items listed, many with lengthy descriptions and color graphics. There is also an abbreviated online version that gives a broad overview of the printed counterpart, including a complete listing of the Splash Pages, Certified Cool, and selected publisher editorial materials. It also contains content for their top items, GEMs of the Month, and featured items from the rest of the catalog.

E-ALERT

THE ONLINE *PREVIEWS* APPEARS ONE WEEK BEFORE THE PRINT CATALOG SO THAT CUSTOMERS CAN GET AN ADVANCED PEEK. IT HAS A SECTION FOR GRAPHIC NOVELS, WITH A PICTURE OF THE COVER ART AND A DESCRIPTION OF THE BOOK, AS WELL AS THE COVER PRICE, NUMBER OF PAGES, AND WHETHER IT IS IN COLOR OR BLACK AND WHITE.

Many publishers find advertising in Diamond's catalog to be a good way of reaching their prospective market. Diamond has many advertising options that you can check out online at ***http://vendor.diamondcomics.com/public***. It is an excellent idea to talk to a representative at Diamond about your marketing strategy and get some insight into what you can do as a creator/publisher to raise the profile of your book. Be sure your contact person at Diamond has a copy of the book and has read it before initiating the conversation.

Cold Cut Distribution (***www.coldcut.com***) is a small California distributor that focuses on independent comics. They may prove to be a very viable option for small publishers who can sometimes get lost in the sheer volume of product sold through a venue such as Diamond Comic Distributors. Please note that they don't use a preorder system. If they like your sample book, they will list it in their catalog and offer it to retailers for purchase.

Cold Cut Distribution sells ad space in its irregularly scheduled catalog, the *Bulletin*, as well as in their semiannual large special catalog, *Cold Cut Prime*. It would be advisable to make sure they will accept your book before contracting for advertising space.

Cold Cut says the *Bulletin* is mailed out a few times a year to over six hundred "independent-friendly retailers who have shown an active interest in promoting, carrying, and stocking independent comics in their stores." Other copies of the *Bulletin* are distributed to retailers at trade shows, during on-site store visits, and through publisher referrals.

Each issue of the *Bulletin* stays in these retail outlets for several months—many place more than one reorder per month—and each order involves at least one pass through the *Bulletin*. Other retailers use the *Bulletin* as a product stocking guide. Advertisements are reserved on a first-come, first-served basis.

Although Cold Cut's policy is to make every effort to place advertisements adjacent to book listings, they ask that you indicate a location if desired but cannot guarantee that exact placement will always occur. Limited space is available for ads in each *Bulletin*.

Ads are black and white only and must be camera ready, as they provide no production services. You may supply camera-ready artwork or send it on CD in TIFF format at 300 dpi. You may also supply them a URL where they can download the ad by e-mailing them the information.

Their ads are quite reasonable, running from a quarter page for $45 to a full page for $100. To access information on their advertising policies and prices, go to ***www.coldcut.com/adrates.html***.

Art by John Bolton, design by Melissa Martin.

ANNE RICE'S
THE WITCHING *HOUR*

SORCERY. SUICIDE. SEDUCTION...

Anne Rice's most terrifying novel is now a 13 issue comic book series from Millennium & Comico. Now on sale here!

▲ A promotional poster for the first issue of *Anne Rice's The Witching Hour.*

The Internet

The Web offers possibilities for self-publishers that were unavailable a few years ago. Part of your strategy for promotion should include obtaining a domain name and setting up a Web site to promote your book. The address for the site should appear on all of your promotional material, such as ads, flyers, posters, letterhead, and business cards. The site content should contain plenty of art, as well as downloadable screensavers and other free items that will help to drive traffic to the site.

Don't forget to include a checkout cart or a means for customers to order the book online. You will want to take advantage of impulse buyers as they browse the art. PayPal offers a reliable way for people to pay for merchandise online and it is easy to set up an account.

If you have the time to do so, you should take the opportunity to create a buzz by listing or mentioning your project in as many online locations as possible. This means signing up at Web sites where comic books, pop culture, and graphic novels are discussed.

Creators and artists can sign up for ComicSpace.com (*www.comicspace.com*) where new projects are announced and galleries created. There are discussion boards, reviews, and industry news, too. It's a great place to showcase your project and get feedback from other creators as well as do self-promotion.

If you plan to upload your book as a Web comic, the Webcomiclist site (*www.theweb comiclist.com*) is for you. They list projects chronologically and have a search engine to help navigate through the over eight thousand titles currently carried on the site.

If you print the book through a print-on-demand publisher, look for one that is affiliated with an online store that can offer your book as part of the agreement. List your project in as many places as you can.

Grovel.org (*www.grovel.org.uk/index.php*) is a United Kingdom-based news and views site but lists plenty of American graphic novels.

Internet giant Yahoo has a site for those interested in graphic novels at *http://dir.yahoo.com/Entertainment/Comics_and_Animation/Comic_Books/Graphic_Novels*. This page also offers sponsored links, which are the equivalent of buying an ad.

Artbomb.net (*www.artbomb.net/home.jsp*) is a site with a great deal of content, reviews, news, and a column by Warren Ellis. It features a page with listings for mail order as well as online comics.

The Comics Worth Reading site (*http://comicsworthreading.com/category/graphic-novel-news*) has graphic novel and comic book news, recommendations, reviews with attitude, and lots of links.

CHAPTER 18

MARKETING AND PROMOTION

Marketing and promotion go hand in glove with advertising, but both can be done effectively without spending a great deal of money. The important thing about marketing is analyzing and identifying the most interesting part of your book—the elements that make it unique and special. Promotion and marketing simply emphasize the connection or aspect of your project that makes it stand out for any reason. Is it topical, relevant, or trendy in any way?

Ashcan Editions

Although press releases and advertising are tried and true approaches to marketing, ashcan editions of your book provide prospective buyers with sneak peeks at the quality of the artwork and writing in context. Ashcans as a marketing tool have grown in popularity as easy access to copying technology has grown over the years. During the golden age of comics, ashcan editions of comics were printed to establish copyright. They often went straight from the printer to the ashcan.

Today, ashcans could be more accurately described as mini or digest comics. They are widely used by independent publishers as both a sales tool and a way of establishing copyright. A digest comic measures 5½ inches wide by 8½ inches high, while a minicomic is 5½ inches high by 4¼ inches wide. These sizes evolved naturally from folding a standard size 8½ × 11 inch sheet of paper in half to make a digest or in quarters for a minicomic. These comics are generally reproduced by photocopying and are a quick and inexpensive means of promotion. Some creators have even made a career for themselves by producing minicomics, like artist Matt Feazell who parlayed his work in *Cynicalman* and *Zot!* into a newspaper strip called *The Amazing Cynicalman*.

Because of the limited page count and small size, it is possible to produce an ashcan edition for a reasonable cost, and you can decide how elaborate or simple it should be. A black-and-white book with lettering and a color cover might be your best compromise when assembling the project. Such an edition will give a good sense of the art and storyline, as well as provide a good overall idea of production values. Keep in mind that ashcans are only ten to twelve pages in length, so it only gives a short, intriguing taste of the overall project.

E-ALERT

SOME ASPECTS OF YOUR PROMOTION AND MARKETING CAN PUSH YOUR PROJECT TO THE FRONT OF THE PACK. A SAVVY SALES PUSH BEGINS WHEN YOU IDENTIFY WHAT MAKES YOUR BOOK UNIQUE, SPECIAL, AND COMPELLING. PRESS RELEASES AND MARKETING CAN LINK YOUR PROJECT TO POPULAR TRENDS AND NEWS.

An excellent tutorial on creating minicomics can be found at *www.artbabe.com/comicsand art/diy/minicomics/Formats.html*. If you want to create a buzz, sending ashcans out as review copies to industry professionals and online comics sites is a good way to showcase the project. Remember to autograph the front cover!

Conventions and Book Signings

Attending conventions and arranging book signings is an important aspect of marketing and promotion. Very often it is possible to arrange to be a guest at local comic book or science-fiction conventions, where ideally you will have a table where you can display promotional material and samples of the book and sign and sell ashcans or printed copies of your graphic novel.

Even if your book production is not completed, you can still produce ashcan editions and attend conventions in an effort to make contacts and network with industry pros, suppliers, retailers, and fans. Although it can be a little overwhelming to attend these events, it helps to bring one of your co-creators or a friend along for moral support. Have some sort of printed promotional material ready to hand out, whether it is an ashcan, flyer, poster, or a simple press release. Have business cards handy at all times. You never know who will be there or when an opportunity may arise to make an important contact. Business cards let other professionals know that you're serious about your project, and more than likely it will find its way into someone's Rolodex or address book. Likewise, collect cards and contact information from people that you meet at these events and follow up with letters, e-mails, and phone calls. If you have printed copies of your graphic novel available, you are on even firmer ground. Cast your net wider and try to attend as many conventions as possible.

If you have confidence in your book, rent a table and set up a book signing. Be prepared to chat and be pleasant to the public, even those who may not necessarily be the most mannerly people.

E-FACT

BRING ALONG PLENTY OF HANDOUT MATERIALS AND BUSINESS CARDS WHENEVER YOU'RE IN THE PUBLIC EYE. STRIVE TO BE CONFIDENT, PROFESSIONAL, AND EXTREMELY COURTEOUS. WORD TRAVELS FAST WHEN PEOPLE ARE UNPROFESSIONAL AT PUBLIC EVENTS. YOUR JOB IS TO CONNECT WITH PEOPLE. YOU ARE STRIVING NOT ONLY TO MAKE AN IMPRESSION, BUT ALSO TO MAKE A GOOD ONE.

Although being gracious in this environment can be a challenge, having a smile for everyone who approaches your table goes a long way toward attracting people and achieving your marketing and promotional goals. Even if you think it may not be worthwhile, the effect of getting yourself out there is cumulative. Perhaps a local TV news crew could be at the convention and provide you with free publicity.

Book signings arranged through your neighborhood comic book shop, local bookstore, or large chain stores are also a way of heightening awareness of your graphic novel. Very often retailers are quite open to allowing creators to appear as guests. They may be willing to provide publicity and space in a prime location in their stores as well as copies of the book for you to sign while you chat with fans and potential customers.

It helps to have some sort of free item to give away at these events, such as signed ashcans or posters. Many creators even prominently display a jar or bowl of candy bars or treats to lure people to the table when nothing else will get them there. It breaks the ice, and once people have accepted something from you they are more apt to ask about or buy your book.

Compiling a list of potential venues in your area and making contact is important. Write a brief letter to the store manager to introduce yourself and the book, and then follow up with a call or a visit. This sort of contact encourages a friendly relationship with the decision-makers, which can affect how the book is racked and featured in their store. It is hard to get into some large chain stores such as Barnes & Noble, B. Dalton, or Books-a-Million, but that doesn't mean you shouldn't make every attempt to do so.

Reviews and Interviews

Getting your book reviewed or the creators interviewed in several places online or in print can help sales a great deal. It also legitimizes the book and gives its creators a higher industry profile. Several good reviews can create a buzz and draw attention to projects in ways that not even expensive advertising can match.

Be careful to choose established and credible publications and Web sites when you are choosing your promotional partners. A few good words about your project in a respected publication far outweighs pages upon pages of copy in a venue no one reads or has ever heard of.

E-ALERT

YOUR LOCAL DAILY OR WEEKLY NEWSPAPER MAY BE HAPPY TO FEATURE A STORY ABOUT YOU, SO IT NEVER HURTS TO SEND A PRESS RELEASE TO THEM AND FOLLOW UP WITH A PHONE CALL. THIS SORT OF CONTACT OFTEN LEADS TO AN INTERVIEW, WHICH CAN DRIVE BUSINESS TO YOUR WEB SITE AND ALSO INTEREST LOCAL BOOKSTORES IN BOOKING A SIGNING.

If you have done thorough research, you will have accumulated a list of people, organizations, and publications that are associated with the comics and graphic novel industry. Analyze the list carefully, singling out people either in print or online who may be in the best position to read and review your book. Also take note of whether these publications or sites feature interviews with small press artists and writers. If you belong to comics newsgroups, chatrooms, and Web sites, then you undoubtedly have several people within your circle of contacts who would be happy to review your book. If you ask this favor of people, be sure to approach them respectfully and thank them for their time and trouble.

Even if you have no personal contacts, it is still possible to get your book reviewed at online sites. The following sites have an online presence and areas where reviews and interviews are featured:

- Strange Haven.com:
  www.strange-haven.com/review/index.html
- Comic Book Resources:
  www.comicbookresources.com
- BlogCritics Magazine:
  http://blogcritics.org/books
- Comics Worth Reading:
  http://comicsworthreading.com
- The Masked Bookwyrm's Graphic Novel Reviews:
  www.geocities.com/SoHo/study/4273/graphic.html
- Diamond Comic Distributors:
  http://bookshelf.diamondcomics.com/public/default.asp?t=1&m=1&c=20&s=158&ai=7075
- No Flying, No Tights:
  www.noflyingnotights.com/index2.html
- Sequential Tart:
  www.sequentialtart.com/archive/jan01/home.shtml

Your Internet Site

It may not have escaped your attention that a Web site is a necessity in today's world for people trying to do business, but this applies to graphic novel publishers and creators. Not only does an online presence open up your project to the world, it can bring the world to your door.

△ Try to be imaginative in your marketing and keep up with the new technology.

A domain name descriptive of your project (think of something really snappy) should be obtained in the early planning stages so that by the time you are ready to launch you will have a Web address to put on your stationery, business cards, and other contact info. If you're not computer savvy, enlisting the assistance of a professional in setting up the pages will save you time and labor.

Your site should contain examples of art, interviews with your creative team, a chat room, links to other comics sites, free downloads such as screensavers or wallpaper featuring your characters, and content related to the project. Last but not least, the site should have a way for people to purchase your graphic novel.

If you already are comfortable with the Internet and have the confidence to tackle the task of Web site creation yourself, you can find a great deal of help on the Internet. The Web Developer's Journal, ***www.webdevelopers journal.com/columns/abcs_of_building_web_sites .html***, is a great site for those wishing to familiarize themselves with what is involved in Web page creation. It explains basic Web concepts and terminology, as well as telling you the top ten things you shouldn't do on your site. Other important issues discussed are Web site promotion, which is something that begins with good Web site design, plus an overview of how search engines work and the role clean design plays in leading to higher rankings on the search engines.

The Build 4u Web Site (***www.buildwebsite4u .com/building/build-website.shtml***) also has lots of good, basic information about site creation and management, as well as a section where several types of site-building software are compared and discussed, including links to some that are free.

Yahoo Business has basic site-hosting templates that are inexpensive and easy to set up at ***http://smallbusiness.yahoo.com/webhosting***. Some merchants opt to upgrade these and hire Web designers to upgrade the template to enhance the search engine rankings.

Just be aware that these designers can end up charging from $1,000–$3,000 for a complete redesign. Is it worth it? Perhaps, if you consider that research shows that consumers make up their minds about a site almost instantly, deciding yes or no about a site within the first few seconds of landing on it.

Consequently, a professional and attractive layout is crucial, and design firms can pretty up Yahoo's utilitarian, barebones templates in many ways. But maybe you can too using reference material such as *The Everything® Blogging Book* by Aliza Sherman Risdah and *The Everything® Online Business Book* by Rob Liflander.

CHAPTER 19

DISTRIBUTION

Although the marketplace for the distribution of the traditional comic has decreased considerably since the early nineties when there were many distributors, today new markets are opening up for graphic novels. They are now considered a legitimate form, showcasing the convergence of various elements from popular culture: movies, videos, books, television, and the Internet. This has led to the perception that graphic novels are mainstream, and not only are they accepted increasingly in libraries, universities, and bookstores, they are even downloadable from the Internet.

Diamond Comic Distributors

From the late 1980s through the mid-1990s, there were more than a dozen comic book distributors in America. Today, Diamond is the only large distributor.

Diamond Comic Distributors is now the world's largest wholesaler for English-language comic and pop-culture related items. In business since 1982, they are the primary avenue of distributing directly to comics shops, who buy products they offer on a nonreturnable basis. Diamond's catalog, *Previews,* lists products from all the major comics producers as well as small presses and independent publishers. Typically, a period of six months will elapse between the time you contact Diamond about distributing your product to the time you receive your payment. The timeline runs like this:

January Initiate contact with Diamond's purchasing department.

February Send your submission package to Diamond for consideration. If accepted, you will work out terms of sale with the purchasing brand manager.

March Your product appears in the *Previews* catalog.

April Diamond compiles retailer orders from the March catalog then generates a purchase order and transmits it to you.

May You ship your product to Diamond, and Diamond then ships it to retailers. You send Diamond an invoice for your products.

June Diamond sends payment for your product.

At their Web site, click on the Vendors tab to download information about submitting your book to them for inclusion in the catalog.

They will ask for your submission package:
- Your proposed terms of sale
- Product samples
- Product information
- Promotional artwork
- Press releases
- Contact information

Key points to remember:
- Diamond asks for a 60–70 percent discount off the cover price of your product.
- It will take six months to receive a check from the time you start the solicitation process with Diamond.
- The publisher pays for shipping from the printer to the nearest Diamond distribution point.

Send a complete copy of your comic in your submissions package. Photocopies are accepted, but, with the exception of advertisements and editorial pages, the book must be complete. They prefer to see a lettered, inked, and, if applicable, a fully colored copy of your book. Diamond asserts that their policy of reviewing the quality of a graphic novel ahead of time assists them with their promotional and editorial decisions. This enables them to carry only professional-looking products, and the submission procedure acts as a screening process to prevent amateurish work from diluting the market. Please note that your art samples will *not* be returned.

Additional data that must be gathered for Diamond's solicitation package should be summarized on one sheet:

- Title
- Issue number and number of issues in series (if applicable)
- Name(s) of creator(s)
- Synopsis
- Intended audience (all ages, mature readers, or adult material)
- Format (color or black and white, size, and page count)
- Retail price
- Printer or shipping-point origin
- Country of origin (where your comics will be printed, not produced)
- Ship date
- Order increase cutoff date (the last day on which you can accept an increase in orders from Diamond, usually shortly before you set your print run)
- UPC code (optional)
- Licensing restrictions (if any)
- Special discount information (if any)

Amazon.com

The publishing world is changing, and the online store Amazon.com (*www.amazon.com*) has been instrumental in changing the face of publishing and distribution. BookSurge, an Amazon.com company, offers complete publishing and online distribution services for independent publishers.

Amazon's online Advantage program is structured so you can list and control your own product page on their Web site. To join you must meet certain criteria: You must own the North American distribution rights for your books, have scannable barcodes with the ISBN on the back cover of the book, and have online access so you can manage your account online. Advantage costs $29.95 per year, plus there is a 55 percent standard commission on the sale of your items.

The more a potential customer knows about your book, the more likely he is to buy it. When you join Amazon.com Advantage, they make it easy for you to include sample passages, customer reviews, cover art, an author bio, and more to your page. When a potential customer visits the page, he can see your book cover, read a sample from it, read about the project's creators, and see customer reviews.

These factors put your product out there on the Internet and allow you to supervise how it is presented to customers. Every customer who clicks on your page drives traffic, which means your book rates higher in recommendations, which in turn helps put your book in front of more potential customers.

Amazon has comprehensive forecasting tools, so your books stay in stock with very low returns. Amazon may initially order as little as two books and keep just enough in stock to fill anticipated customer orders. They will adjust the number of copies they order based on recent sales performance, and when inventory runs low they will automatically send you an e-mail requesting more copies.

Amazon.com handles the payment, shipping, and all customer service issues, including returns. At the end of each month they automatically pay you for the copies that sold during the previous month—without invoicing. Payment can be made to you via electronic funds transfer (EFT) or check. All sales, inventory, and payment information is online in your Advantage account, so you can always check to see how your items are selling and how much money is owed.

Bookstores

In these days of megastores, it is not impossible to get your book carried by a large book chain, but it does require quite a bit of preparation and work.

The bricks-and-mortar superstore giants such as Borders, Barnes & Noble, B. Dalton, Waldenbooks, and Books-A-Million will not accept a book that doesn't have an ISBN number and a barcode. They carry so many products that they must be able to do inventory control rapidly by scanning barcodes and tracking by ISBN numbers. The Web site for the ISBN agency is *www.ISBN.org*, phone 877-310-7333. Allow ten days for processing a request for an ISBN, unless you are willing to pay an extra fee for rush handling. If your book has already been printed, you can sticker it with the ISBN once it has been assigned. The ISBN and price should appear on the back cover of the book.

The bar code that incorporates your ISBN is scanned at the time of purchase, thus recording accurately the sale of your book. The book industry uses the Bookland EAN bar code, not the UPC. If your book is already printed, you have pressure-sensitive labels produced for placement on the back cover. For a list of commercial bar code suppliers, visit the BISG Web site: *www.bisg.org/barcoding/bc_suppliers.html.*

Barnes & Noble has a few more suggestions for small publishers. They say your willingness to place the book with a book wholesaler may determine whether they carry it. Although wholesalers normally expect a 50–55 percent discount, they pay in sixty to ninety days and expect books to be returnable.

Placing your book with a wholesaler will simplify your billing and allows B&N to consider placing larger orders plus put the book on automatic replenishment status. As Bookstar and B. Dalton are subsidiaries of Barnes & Noble, expect similar policies from them as well as the other superstores. To request consideration for store placement, Barnes & Noble asks that you submit a finished copy of the book along with your marketing and promotion strategies, trade reviews, and a brief note describing what makes the book unique to:

The Small Press Department
Barnes & Noble, Inc.
122 Fifth Avenue
New York, NY 10011
212-633-3388 (general information)
212-463-5677 (fax)

They require that you also include the ISBN and the suggested retail price. The review process takes about six weeks, and their Small Press Department responds to all submissions in writing. The following site has more helpful information for writers and publishers: *www.barnesandnoble.com/help/cds2.asp?PID=8149&z=y&cds2Pid=8148*.

Borders has almost identical requirements, and their information can be found at: *https://www.bordersstores.com/care/care.jsp?page=10#placement*. To have your book reviewed for stock selection in a Borders or Waldenbooks store, they require a copy of the book along with a completed Product Submission Form.

The Product Submission Form is found at *https://www.bordersstores.com/data/bstores/features/pdfs/product_submission_sheet.pdf*. They will not consider submissions that do not include the form. Send your book and the form to:

New Vendor Acquisitions
Borders Group, Inc.
100 Phoenix Drive
Ann Arbor, MI 48108

Your submission will be reviewed by their buyers and considered for placement in their stores or listing for customer special orders.

Borders makes a point of saying that the use of a distributor or wholesaler factors into their decision on whether to carry a book. They believe there are advantages to be gained by both the publisher and retailers when wholesalers and distributors are used.

Books submitted will not be returned, and your submission will only be acknowledged if the buyer wishes to purchase it and they cannot obtain it through a vendor that they trade with. A list of these vendors can be found at: *https://www.bordersstores.com/data/bstores/features/pdfs/suggested_wholesalers_06212006.pdf*.

Contact independently owned bookstores in your area about carrying your graphic novel. Most of these stores are very supportive of local authors and will be happy to work with you and carry your graphic novel.

Cold Cut Distribution and Alternative Distributors

Distributors that specialize in independent and alternative comics aren't too numerous, but there are a few out there that are definitely worth contacting. Cold Cut may be among the largest of the independent distributors, but contact information and background information for other distributors are included in the following sections.

COLD CUT DISTRIBUTION
220 N. Main Street
Salinas, CA 93901
Phone: 831-751-7300
Fax: 831-751-1513
E-mail: orders@coldcut.com
*Web: **www.coldcut.com***

Cold Cut is a wholesale distributor of small press, independent, and alternative graphic novels and comic books to both comics retailers and bookstores. Cold Cut Distribution states they are the industry's leading reorder distributor for quality independent comics. They offer instant reorders on thousands of titles from more than two hundred different independent publishers, all at very competitive reorder discounts that may match or beat the prices of the bigger distributors. Cold Cut claims that their discounts are the best in the industry, with no additional reorder charges. They have a top discount level of 50 percent and a 90 percent rebate on shipping on larger-sized orders.

The first step in determining whether they will accept your product is to send a sample copy of your book to their Submissions Director. You will be contacted about the terms and conditions.

You can also e-mail them at *comics@ coldcut.com* to follow up a week or two after you have sent in your sample. Be aware that they do not carry everything, however. They note on their site that although their policies are more liberal than Diamond's, and in particular they favor alternative comics that Diamond often overlooks, there are some books they have trouble selling, such as those featuring superheroes. For books that they do decide to pick up, they usually start off with a rather small order of ten to twenty copies to gauge retailer interest. For further information on submissions contact the submissions director at the address given previously.

LAST GASP
777 Florida Street
San Francisco, CA 94110
Phone: 800-366-5121

Last Gasp (*www.lastgasp.com*) is primarily a publisher, but they also have a distribution division. In the 1960s they started out as publishers of underground comics, and now they are one of the largest publishers and sellers of underground comics in the world. They also act as a distributor of all sorts of literature, graphic novels, and art books. Their graphic novels Web page (*www.lastgasp.com/1/1/160*) lists over 1,500 titles.

To submit your project to Last Gasp for distribution and for inclusion in their newsletters and on their Web site, send a nonreturnable review copy to the attention of the submissions department at the aforementioned address.

They choose items for distribution that fit into their market niche: the unusual, the alternative, and out-of-the-ordinary materials. Since everyone is a multitasker at Last Gasp, they ask for your patience in getting a response as it sometimes takes a little longer than they would like to get back to you. To receive a response, you must include a self-addressed stamped envelope. They ask that you wait three to four weeks before following up with a phone call after you've sent in a review copy.

Their discount level is 60 percent off the cover price; books are resold to stores at 40 to 55 percent off cover price.

INGRAM BOOK COMPANY

One Ingram Boulevard
Post Office Box 3006
La Vergne, TN 37086-1986

According to the Ingram Book Group, they try to keep up with nearly two hundred continuing graphic novel series as well as stand-alones. Ingram and its partner, POD publisher Lightning Source, offer a listing in a digital catalog. The catalog is a powerful tool for publishers, providing them with the mechanism for getting their books listed with the largest wholesalers, retailers, and distributors in the book industry.

They charge a digital catalog fee of $12.00 per year, which entitles a publisher to the following services:

- Detailed title listings in all daily catalogs Lightning Source provides to its U.S. distribution partners, such as Ingram and Baker & Taylor
- Detailed title listing in all daily catalogs Lightning Source provides to its international distribution partners, such as Bertrams and Gardners
- Title summary included in their bibliographic catalog feed
- Thumbnail cover image preparation and inclusion in their bibliographic catalog feed
- Storage and backup of both title content and bibliographic data
- Price and discount maintenance for publisher price changes

Ingram recently announced that it would only be handling publishers who have a roster of ten titles or more. They have posted a list of smaller distributors through which they order at ***www.ingrambook.com/new/distributors.asp***.

This site has listings for many distributors with links to their Web sites, which list their policies and requirements and contact information. Most seem to have a relationship with Baker & Taylor, Ingram, Barnes & Noble, Amazon, and Borders.

BAKER & TAYLOR

Baker & Taylor is the number-one book supplier to libraries, which seem to be increasingly open to stocking graphic novels and manga. Contact the Ordering Department at 251 Mt. Olive Church Road, Commerce, GA 30599-1100 (***www.btol.com/images/email/Html/PI_viewhere.html***) or phone 800-937-8200.

B&T services two types of markets. Its main business distributes books, calendars, music, and DVDs to schools and libraries worldwide, while the firm's retail unit supplies storefront and Internet retailers and independent booksellers with some four million book titles. They do have a graphic novel and manga buyer, a resident expert on all things illustrated, who puts together lists of new and forthcoming titles with valuable commentary on several of the most highly anticipated titles.

Mail Order and Internet Download

The best financial return publishers see on their investment is usually through mail order or Internet sales. Your Web site is the perfect place to offer a description, photos, and an easy means of ordering your graphic novel. Provide the customer with a way of immediately checking out and purchasing your book through online means such as PayPal or a credit card. A last resort would be to accept checks through the mail—when people want a product they want the immediate gratification of having their order processed and knowing the book will be in the mail within days.

For those who are afraid of transactions on the Internet, ordering your book by mail is a viable option. It is slower for them and you as you must wait for the check to clear, and that delays their book getting shipped out.

Independent and small press publishers have to grasp the enormous potential of developing an online presence so they can keep the majority of the profits rather than pay a middleman such as a wholesaler or distributor. If you can partner with online sites that sell a downloadable version of your book, or if you can create such a site for yourself, you will vastly increase your profit margin.

A cleverly designed Web site will feature art samples to intrigue the potential reader and free downloadable screensavers and wallpaper to attract readers to the site. If they like what they see, you can capitalize on the impulse buying instinct and offer a quick PayPal checkout option.

Adobe Acrobat files convert text and graphics into a file format called PDF (Portable Document Format). CBR stands for Comic Book Reader, and this format allows you to download a book and read it at your leisure, too.

TalkAboutComics.com has an interesting discussion and demonstration of CBR at *www.talkaboutcomics.com/blog/index.php?cat=4*. Go to this link for a free download for the CDisplay software. CDisplay (*www.geocities.com/davidayton/CDisplay*) is sequential image-viewing software that allows you to display CBR files.

A cover price significantly lower than that of the printed version makes the download extra appealing. Don't be greedy; a significant discount will boost sales. Remember: You don't have to pay printing or distribution costs, so you can afford to be generous.

Some online sites offer downloads and/or sales of printed books. This means that a digital version is available to read for a fee or for free, or that it is possible to order the book from an online catalog. A short list of online resources includes:

- Mile High Comics:
  www.milehighcomics.com/istore/indsmp.html
- The Webcomiclist:
  www.thewebcomiclist.com/suggest.php
- DriveThruComics:
  http://comics.drivethrustuff.com/catalog/index.php
- Web Comics Nation:
  www.webcomicsnation.com

CHAPTER 20

LEGALITIES

As you have created your graphic novel, you have followed a path through a tangle of production procedures and marketing challenges. By tackling them in logical order and sticking to a plan, ideally you have created a unique work. To protect what you have created and reap the benefits of your labors, you must now take the steps necessary to legally protect your creation and the business insfrastructure that supports it.

Copyrights and Trademarks

Although your work is recognized as being copyrighted from the moment you complete it in tangible form, the law doesn't cover the actual concept or ideas. Since 1989, copyright is automatic and therefore it is not absolutely necessary to have your work registered with the copyright office. However, registration does serve as evidence of a valid ownership and entitles the owner of the work to seek damages in the case of infringement.

Placing a copyright notation, such as the © symbol, next to the title of your work or spelling it out in the ownership and publication information of your novel, such as "Copyright 2008, William B. Williams," will suffice as legal notice of ownership. However, if you choose to register your work with the copyright office, you can check out the qualifications and steps and get downloadable forms by visiting the U.S. Copyright Office's Web site at *www.copyright.gov* or by calling 202-707-3000 for more information.

Another aspect of copyright law you should be aware of is the work-for-hire arrangement. This would pertain to you if an artist was commissioned to produce the illustrations for your graphic novel. Unless you are engaged in a partnership arrangement, you must draw up a contract or some other written instrument that specifies you hold complete ownership of the property and that other contributions were created under a work-for-hire agreement.

A written contract that spells out the nature of a work-for-hire agreement is necessary for it to be recognized as legally binding. An old axiom about copyright law in general states that "a verbal contract isn't worth the paper it's printed on."

Fair use describes the use of a copyrighted work for purposes such as criticism, commentary, news reporting, teaching (including multiple copies for classroom use), scholarship, or research. Fair use is not considered an infringement of copyright. In determining whether the use made of a work in any particular case is indeed fair use, these factors need to be considered:

- The purpose and character of the use, including whether such use is of a commercial nature or is for nonprofit educational purposes
- The nature of the copyrighted work
- The amount of the portion used in relation to the copyrighted work as a whole
- The effect of the use upon the potential market for or value of the copyrighted work

E-ALERT

AT ONE TIME A SYSTEM KNOWN AS THE "POOR MAN'S COPYRIGHT" WAS POPULAR. THIS ENTAILED PUTTING A COPY OF THE WORK IN A SEALED ENVELOPE AND MAILING IT TO YOURSELF VIA CERTIFIED OR REGISTERED MAIL. BE AWARE THAT THIS PRACTICE IS NOT LEGALLY RECOGNIZED AS HAVING THE SAME STANDING AS REGISTERING YOUR WORK WITH THE U.S. COPYRIGHT OFFICE.

Trademarks are distinctive signs used by an individual, business organization, or other entity to uniquely establish the sole source of its products, characters, and even services. A trademark comprises a name, word, phrase, logo, symbol, design, image, or a combination of these elements. For example, although DC Comics cannot copyright the word *superman*, they are able to claim it as a trademark when it is appears in conjuction with the recognizable Superman logo. How many times have you seen this distinctive trademark copied? It has been imitated to hype everything from mattresses to automobiles.

As with copyrights, the law considers trademarks to be a matter of intellectual property, but unlike copyrights, anyone wanting to claim a trademark must file through the U.S. Patent and Trademark Office (*www.uspto.gov*). The process is considerably more expensive and time-consuming than copyright registration.

Legal registration of a trademark must meet a number of different criteria before it can be granted. The law in most jurisdictions allows the owner of a registered trademark to prevent unauthorized use. These rights are generally only enforceable in that jurisdiction, a characteristic that is sometimes known as *territoriality*. Trademarking the title logo of your graphic novel isn't necessary to make a legally recognized claim for ownership.

Ancillary Rights

Whether you are the writer, the artist, or the creator of copyrighted intellectual property, you own what the law refers to as a *bundle of rights* that comprise the property, from primary to secondary or subsidiary rights. What is defined as those rights varies depending on the initial form you choose for your work.

In the particular example of a graphic novel, other rights automatically covered by copyright law are the film (screen and TV) and audio adaptation rights. These rights are not "book" rights (hard and soft cover); they are what are often referred to as subsidiary or ancillary rights.

The distinction between the two isn't really relevant, since your copyrighted graphic novel is legally recognized with precise particularity in regards to *all* your rights as the property's owner. Sale or use of your ancillary rights remains your sole prerogative. Partial or complete copyright ownership can only be transferred through an assignment or license.

Today's creators of graphic novels often have the ancillary market in mind when conceptualizing their project as the trend toward the adaptation of graphic novels to the screen continues. The market for subsidiary rights will rapidly expand as more graphic novels become video games and Web comics.

Royalties

A *royalty* is a percentage of the wholesale price of a graphic novel that a publisher pays to the copyright owner in exchange for the right to copy and distribute that work. Royalties are often based on the number of units sold. If you are the sole creator of all aspects of the graphic novel, then you are entitled to receive royalties from your publisher based on the contract you signed, presuming you did not self-publish. If you have a royalty agreement with a partner (such as an artist) for those rights, you will share a percentage of the revenue with the partner. If you enter into negotiations to license the subsidiary rights to another party, such as a film studio, then it's advisable to seek out professional counsel regarding a royalty rate. Ideally, you should consult an attorney who practices intellectual property law, which is extremely nuanced and open to interpretation.

Often what seems like innocuous language in a contract can turn out to be a costly mistake for the creator. As the old saying goes, the devil is in the details. If someone approaches you offering to license your property for adaptation in any medium, great care should be taken before signing any legal document. This cannot be stressed too much. An attorney should look over any contract that you sign to ensure that your interests as to royalties and intellectual property rights are protected.

The most legendary costly mistake in the history of the comics field was made by Joe Shuster and Jerry Siegel when they sold their rights to Superman for under three hundred dollars. It required numerous court cases and forty years before that error in judgment was rectified, and all of the permutations of that seventy-year-old decision have yet to be worked out.

Public Domain

Ironically, there is now a publication that discusses many aspects of intellectual property law in comic book form. *Tales from the Public Domain: Bound by Law?* is the kitschy title. This little pamphlet talks about copyright law as it pertains to filmmaking and is an interesting juxtaposition of graphic images and legalese. It can be downloaded from the Duke Law School site at *www.law.duke.edu/cspd/comics*.

The *Wall Street Journal* says: "*Bound by Law* translates law into plain English and abstract ideas into 'visual metaphors.' So the comic's heroine, Akiko, brandishes a laser gun as she fends off a cyclopean 'Rights Monster'—all the while learning copyright law basics, including the line between fair use and copyright infringement." The Duke Law School site's Center for the Study of the Public Domain (*www.law.duke.edu/cspd*) explores some fascinating topics and is worth checking out.

Art by Rik Levins, *Nosferatu Plague of Darkness* © 2006 Mark Ellis.

◀ The image of the Nosferatu was first imprinted in public consciousness through an unlicensed film adaptation in 1922 of Bram Stoker's *Dracula*. Now, both Dracula and Nosferatu are in public domain.

Cornell University's Copyright Information Center (*www.copyright.cornell.edu/training/Hirtle_ Public_Domain.htm*) has a chart that shows the timetable and requirements for works considered to be in the public domain. This reference chart shows the many permutations of whether a work is in the public domain or not with all the many variables as to date, published with or without copyright notice, and country of origin listed.

E-FACT

SUPERBOY IS CURRENTLY THE SUBJECT OF A LEGAL BATTLE BETWEEN TIME WARNER, THE OWNER OF DC COMICS, AND THE ESTATE OF JERRY SIEGEL. THE SIEGELS ARGUE THAT THE SUPERBOY CHARACTER WAS CONCEIVED SEPARATELY FROM SUPERMAN AND THEREFORE WAS NOT PART OF THE RIGHTS INITIALLY SOLD TO DC. A SUMMARY JUDGMENT IN *2004* RULED THAT THE SIEGEL HEIRS HAD THE RIGHT TO REVOKE DC'S COPYRIGHT ASSIGNMENT TO SUPERBOY AND SUCCESSFULLY RECLAIM THE RIGHTS.

Interestingly, German filmmaker F. W. Murnau based his silent film *Nosferatu* on Bram Stoker's *Dracula* without permission. Since the film first appeared in 1922, all aspects of it have fallen into the public domain. The unique design for the title character has been borrowed for many vampire films and books.

Record-keeping

Organization for your project started when you were in the planning stages and you began to chart production flow in order to be able to schedule things properly. It continued when you shopped around for a printer and went forward into the marketing, promotion, and distribution phases. Hopefully you bought a planner/calendar or PDA early in this endeavor and update and check it frequently.

You may not be aware of the many tools to help people keep track of work flow and expenses, but whatever you use, good record-keeping is vital. Investing in a file cabinet, book-shelves, and folders is the first rudimentary step. Every penny that you spend for supplies, not only to create the project but also to manage the business end of it, is tax deductible.

A bulletin board where you post notes and memos, hung in a prominent place, is a good way of keeping things that need your immediate attention. After a while you will more than likely use the same software or ledger book to record income derived from book sales. Don't forget that the following should all have a file folder to track expenses for tax deductions or just to be at hand for easy reference:

- Notes and ideas concerning the project. Having a folder where you can file notes, inspirations, and sudden insights saves time and feeds the muse.
- Business receipts. Reference materials used in the creation and/or marketing of your work are tax deductible. Office equipment such as furniture and computer equipment can be deducted and/or depreciated, too. Your receipts folder should ideally have subfolders or divisions within it that designate categories such as office supplies, art supplies, utility bills, and postage.
- Information on printers. This should be kept with quotes for the book and promotional material plus notes you made during contact.

- A list of comics and graphic novel-related Web sites that are of particular interest to the project.
- A list of contacts that have not only street addresses, phone numbers, fax numbers, and e-mail addresses but also the name(s) and business titles of contacts. This list is easily kept on the computer, but a hard copy should always be printed and stored in a safe place.
- A list of places to market and promote the book derived from the Web and other sources.
- A list of distributors, with details of their terms and conditions.

If you use bookkeeping software, inputting this data every month is a good backup in case a receipt gets lost or misfiled. It is also great to have this data in a program such as Excel or QuickBooks when you do your taxes. In any event, if you don't use a software program to track expenses and income, this information should be recorded in a ledger book where you make a record of monthly expenses.

Thorough record-keeping saves hours of lost time that you can put to better use. Most importantly, always back up computer files onto a separate disk or hard drive. You'll be glad you did, because it is worth the time and effort to achieve peace of mind.

GLOSSARY

Adobe Photoshop: The world's most popular software program for processing and manipulating images.

alignment: A typographical term that describes the type's orientation on the left, center, or right of the page. See *flush left*, *flush center*, and *flush right*.

Ames Lettering Guide: A small plastic tool used to draw guidelines and spaces to facilitate hand lettering dialogue and captions on a page.

ashcans: A minicomic used for promotional purposes and to establish copyright.

balloons: An oval shape containing lettering that points to the speaker. There are both word and thought balloons.

bar code: An identifying number or ISBN placed on the back of a book so that it can be tracked.

baseline: A typographic term for the straight, imaginary line on which letters sit.

bleed: An image, graphic, or ink coverage that extends up to or past the edge of the page.

bricks-and-mortar store: A term used to differentiate real stores from their online counterparts.

Bristol board: Heavyweight paper used for penciling and inking.

bursts: A jagged-edge balloon that may contain sound effects or shouted dialogue.

byte: A unit of measure equivalent to 8 bits.

caps: Uppercase or capital letters.

caption: The lettering that describes action or a scene in a comics panel.

caricature: An illustration style that exaggerates features for humorous effect.

character: A fictional element that exists inside a story, not necessarily always a person.

CMYK: Cyan, magenta, yellow, and black. Ink colors used in four-color printing to create all the other colors.

color separations: Separating the color elements of an image in such a way as to make them printable. They are made up of four sheets of film: cyan, magenta, yellow, and black.

comic: A book that uses sequential art to tell a story.

comic strip: A cartoon that uses a sequence of panels to tell a story.

computer-to-plate (CTP): A printing technology where the image is burned by laser onto the printing plate, eliminating the need for film.

copyright: The legal claim to an image and its usage.

Corel Painter: A software program used by colorists.

cross-hatching: A drawing method using inked lines drawn in close proximity to one another to produce a shadowed effect.

dingbat: A typographical term for a nonalphanumeric image used for decorative effect.

distributor: A wholesaler who acts as middleman between the publisher and sales outlets.

double-page spread: Two full pages of art (known as splashes) printed side by side to make one continuous image.

download: Using one's computer to take a file from an Internet site.

dpi: Dots per inch, a way of describing image quality. The more dpi, the higher the image resolution and quality, and the larger the file size.

Dr. Martin's Dyes: Concentrated watercolor inks used to color comics.

e-zine: An online magazine.

flatting: A digital coloring term for filling large areas with color.

flush center: A typographic term for placing type in the center of the page.

flush left: A typographic term for aligning type on the left margin.

flush right: A typographic term for aligning type on the right margin.

folding dummy: A guide for printers that shows the sequence the pages should appear in a print project.

font: A style of type with distinctive characteristics.

force or speed lines: Short parallel lines used to give the impression of movement or speed.

foreshortening: A drawing technique in which the objects closest to the viewer are drawn larger than ones that recede into the background.

full script: A script in which all dialogue is complete and all plot details and actions are laid out panel by panel. Art direction is also included.

GIF: A graphic image format used for small images used on the Internet.

gigabyte (GB): One thousand megabytes.

grayscale: An image made of 256 shades of gray, from black to white.

halftone: An image composed of dots of various sizes that blend together to represent a continuous-tone image.

gutter: The space between panels on a comics page.

hits: The number of visits made to a Web site.

horizon: The horizontal line in perspective drawing that is always at the viewer's eye level.

hue: A specific color designation, such as red, blue, yellow.

illustrated novel: A graphic novel presented almost exclusively through captions, without word balloons.

image area: The printable area on a page.

imposed: Also called imposition. A printing term used to described the order in which pages are sequenced.

independent comics: Sometimes called indies. Any comic or graphic novel produced by smaller publishers.

inking: The process by which a line is laid down over pencils in ink using a pen or brush.

ISBN: Abbreviation for *International Standard Book Number*, a unique identifying number recognized and used internationally wherever books are sold commercially.

ISP: Internet service provider. The company that provides Internet service to the customer.

JPEG: A compressed file format for images and graphics.

kicker: An event at the bottom of a page so compelling or interesting that it motivates the reader to turn to the next page.

kilobyte (K): One thousand bytes of data.

layout: A representation of a final printed piece that shows the placement of all the design elements.

leading: A typographic term that describes the distance between the baselines in text.

lettering: The process of adding text to pages, done by hand or on the computer, usually in the form of word balloons or captions.

line art: The product of inking penciled lines to produce a black line image.

lines per inch (lpi): The number of rows of dots that comprise an image.

manga: Japanese comic books, often made into cartoons, or anime. The art in manga has a very specific look to it and is immediately recognizable.

marketing: Presenting a project to the public by diverse means, including advertising.

Marvel Method: A technique for creating a comic where the penciler is provided with the basic plot, either as a detailed synopsis or general overview, and then interprets the story as he or she thinks best, breaking it down into panels and pages.

megabyte (MB): 1,048,576 bytes, or 1,024 kilobytes of data.

megastore: A large national chain, such as Barnes & Noble.

minimalistic design: A design that is simplified and streamlined, lacking detail.

moiré: A distortion of halftone dots that produces a pattern within the halftone area.

narrative flow: A story that describes a sequence of events caused and experienced by the characters.

negative space: An area deliberately left blank for design purposes, usually later filled with lettering or a sound effect.

nonrepro blue: A shade of blue that graphics cameras can't capture, used to define printed page grids and sometimes used by pencilers to draw images on pages.

off model: An animation term that describes a character's drawing that does not follow the pre-scribed original source material or model sheets, often as a form of parody.

pacing: The speed and rhythm at which a story moves.

panel: A box or shape used to define areas in sequential art.

penciling: The initial step in creating a page layout in pencil.

perfect binding: A printing term for a book with pages that are held together with adhesive, such as most paperback books. It has a flat spine with text usually imprinted on it.

perspective: The representation on a two-dimensional surface (paper) of a three-dimensional object so that it appears realistic to the human eye.

pica: A unit of measure used by printers and typographers, equal to 12 points or 1/6 inch.

plot: The ordering of scenes and action within a story, the narrative that drives the work.

point: A measurement used by typographers and printers to measure the size of type, equal to 1/72 of an inch.

print on demand: A printing process in which a copy isn't printed until an order is received (abbreviated POD).

process color: Refers both to the printing process that uses CMYK colors to reproduce color images and to the colors that are printed using that method.

promotion: A means of getting the project positioned in the market for higher sales.

proof: An example the printer provides the customer to show how the job will print.

resolution: The quality and sharpness of an image derived from the dpi or lpi.

RGB: The colors red, green, and blue. A color mode computers use to display images onscreen.

royalty: A percentage of profit paid on the sale of a property.

sans serif font: A typographic term for a font without extra protrusions, or serifs.

scanning: Using a scanner to turn art into a digitized image.

screen: A dot pattern placed over an area to give the appearance of a shade.

scripter: The writer who creates the plot, characters, and story.

search engine: Sites such as Google, Ask.com, and Yahoo that allow the user to find Internet sites that contain certain keywords or phrases.

serif font: A typography term for fonts that use little protrusions, or serifs, to alter their design.

silhouette: A shadow outline of a person or object with no detail.

sound effect: A short burst of letters that conveys an impression of sound, for example, BLAM!, POW!, and KA-BOOM!

splash page: A single-panel page that usually appears at the beginning of a book, so spectacular that it draws the reader into the story.

stippling: An inking technique that uses dots to convey shades and a gradient of black to white.

subplots: A secondary story or plot line that may or may not connect to the main plot.

synopsis: A brief, condensed version of a story.

T-square: A tool used by artists and inkers to ensure horizontal lines and type are straight and parallel on the pages. Usually used in conjunction with a triangle.

talking heads: A series of panels that contain only the heads of the characters and dialogue. To be avoided whenever possible.

thumbnail breakdown system: A scripting technique in which the writer provides a rough sketch of each page, showing different perspectives and indicating dialogue-balloon placement, to achieve the best balance between text and visuals.

thumbnails: Small sketches that briefly describe an image. Also a very small version of a large photograph.

TIFF: A digital image file format used in graphics and photography.

trademark: A symbol, design, or word protected by law for exclusive use of its owner.

triangle: A tool used by artists and inkers to ensure vertical lines are straight and parallel on the pages. Usually used in conjunction with a T-square.

typography: A printing term derived from calligraphy now used to describe the expert use and design of type.

upload: Using a computer to send files to an Internet site.

vanishing point: A trick of perspective drawing, the point toward which all lines seem to converge and disappear.

vernacular: A local dialect, accent, or regional way of speaking.

VoIP: Abbreviation for *voice over Internet protocol*. Making telephone calls over the Internet.

Web comic: A comic book or graphic novel that is placed on the Web for viewing or downloading.

widows: In typography, a word or two or part of a sentence at the end of a paragraph that is carried over to the top of the following page.

World Wide Web (WWW): An international network of computers linked to form an immense database of information that can be accessed via computer.

wraparound cover: Front cover art and design that is carried over to the back cover.

zipped: A digital file that has been compressed so it can be easily sent over the Internet or stored.

ADDITIONAL RESOURCES

Print Resources

The Comic Book Heroes, Gerard Jones and Will Jacobs, Prima Publishing, 1997

Comics Crash Course, Vince Giarrano, Impact Books, 2004

DC Comics: Sixty Years of the World's Favorite Comic Book Heroes, Les Daniels, Bulfinch Press, 1991

Draw Comics with Dick Giordano, Dick Giordano, Impact Books, 2005

The Everything Drawing Book, Helen South, Adams Media, 2005

The History of Comics Volumes One and Two, Jim Steranko, Supergraphics, 1972

How to Draw Manga, Hikaru Hayashi, Graphic-Sha, 2003

Marvel: Five Fabulous Decades of the World's Greatest Comics, Les Daniels, Marvel Entertainment Group, 1991

Online Resources

American Library Association
www.ala.com

Cellar Door Publishing
www.cellardoorpublishing.com

Checker Book Publishing Group
www.checkerbpg.com

Top Shelf Productions
www.topshelfcomix.com

Comicbook Artists' Guild
www.comicartguild.com

Comic Book Art Supplies
www.comicartistsupplies.com

Comic Book Conventions
www.comicbookconventions.com

Comic Book Legal Defense Fund
www.cbldf.org

Comicraft
www.comicraft.com

Comics Buyer's Guide
www.cbgxtra.com

ComicSpace
www.comicspace.com

Comics2Film
www.comics2film.com

Comixtalk
www.comixpedia.com

ComiXpress
www.comixpress.com

Dark Horse Comics
www.darkhorse.com

DC Comics
www.dccomics.com

Grand Comic Book Database
www.comics.org/

Ka-blam: Print on Demand
www.ka-blam.com

How to Draw Manga: Manga University
www.howtodrawmanga.com

Mark Ellis
www.MarkEllisInk.com

Marvel Comics
www.marvel.com

Melissa Martin Ellis
www.mellissart.com

Plan Nine Publishing
www.plan9.org

Publishers Weekly
www.publishersweekly.com

Superhero Hype
www.superherohype.com

U.S. Copyright Office
www.copyright.gov

Write Now! magazine
http://twomorrows.com/index.php?cPath=60

Wizard magazine
www.wizarduniverse.com/magazine/wizard

ART INDEX

PAGE 2
New Fun #1

PAGE 5
Comics Code Seal

PAGE 10
Satellite in Space

PAGE 3
"Flash" Lightning

PAGE 7
Gangsters

PAGE 11
Historical Accuracy

PAGE 4
Milton Caniff

PAGE 8
World-Building

PAGE 12
Character Research

PAGE 25
Exposing Secrets

PAGE 27
Setting

PAGE 29
Chronology

PAGE 26
Exaggeration

PAGE 28
Street Scene

PAGE 31
The Peregrine

PAGE 26
Jason Redquill

PAGE 29
Timeline

PAGE 34
Superheroes

PAGE 35
New Justice Machine

PAGE 38
Crime Story

PAGE 40
Fantasy

PAGE 36
Facial Expressions

PAGE 39
Imaginative Elements

PAGE 41
Horror

PAGE 36
Fight Scenes

PAGE 39
Death Hawk & Cyke

PAGE 42
Monstahs!

PAGE 43
Explorers

PAGE 50
Paladin Script

PAGE FOUR:

Panel 1: Med. close view of PA's left hand and

ROGUE o/p(1): Long have I coveted your gaunt
Terran ancestors coveted Arthur's Excalibur or

Panel 2: ROGUE walks closer to PA.

ROGUE(2): But unlike those fabled objects of p
nature, not mystical.

(3): I theorize that its energies exist in a "ti
when it was a primal monobloc with no dimensi

PAGE 52
Thumbnails

PAGE 45
Biography

PAGE 51
Paladin Alpha

PAGE 53
Finished Page

PAGE 48
Duelist

PAGE 52
Whisperer

PAGE 56
Lakota

PAGE 57
Layout

PAGE 64
Miskatonic Project

PAGE 70
Character Design

PAGE 61
Talking Heads

PAGE 65
Sound Effects

PAGE 70
Larger Than Life

PAGE 63
Lot No. 249

PAGE 68
Page Design

PAGE 71
Character Types

PAGE 71
Model Sheet

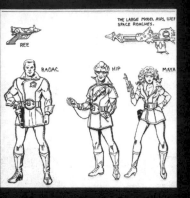

PAGE 74
Double Page Spread

PAGE 77
Historical Period

PAGE 71
Morally Ambiguous

PAGE 76
Computers

PAGE 78
Orbit

PAGE 72
Splash Page

PAGE 77
Prince Valiant

PAGE 79
Art & Text

PAGE 80
Dialogue & Captions

PAGE 83
Anger

PAGE 90
Anatomy

PAGE 81
Redundancy

PAGE 87
Linework

PAGE 91
Perspective

PAGE 82
Tension

PAGE 89
Developing Style

PAGE 92
Expressive

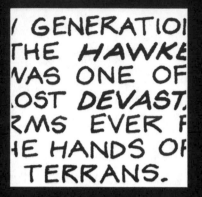

PAGE 108
Pencils

PAGE 110
Inked Paladin

PAGE 113
Cthulhu Inks

PAGE 108
Inked Pencils

PAGE 111
Line Weights

PAGE 113
Stippling Effect

PAGE 110
Penciled Paladin

PAGE 112
Detailed Linework

PAGE 114
Gray Wash

PAGE 116
Dr. Martin's Dyes

PAGE 118
Restrained Palette

PAGE 123
Gouache Coloring

PAGE 117
Computer Color

PAGE 120
B&W Lakota

PAGE 123
Painted Miskatonic

PAGE 118
Scanned Paladin

PAGE 120
Colored Lakota

PAGE 132
Inked Lineart

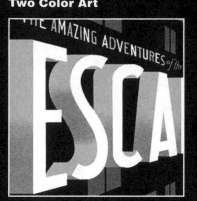
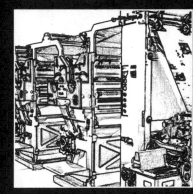

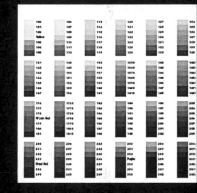

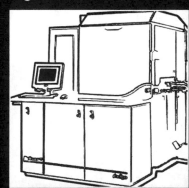

PAGE 156
Damaged Artwork

PAGE 157
Restored Artwork

PAGE 160
Ad Design

PAGE 161
Poster Design

PAGE 162
Cthulhu Ad

PAGE 163
Mummy Poster

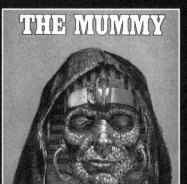

PAGE 165
CBG Ad

PAGE 168
Witching Hour **Poster**

PAGE 175
Thought Balloon

INDEX

THE EVERYTHING SERIES!

BUSINESS & PERSONAL FINANCE

Everything® Accounting Book
Everything® Budgeting Book
Everything® Business Planning Book
Everything® Coaching and Mentoring Book, 2nd Ed.
Everything® Fundraising Book
Everything® Get Out of Debt Book
Everything® Grant Writing Book
Everything® Guide to Foreclosures
Everything® Guide to Personal Finance for Single Mothers
Everything® Home-Based Business Book, 2nd Ed.
Everything® Homebuying Book, 2nd Ed.
Everything® Homeselling Book, 2nd Ed.
Everything® Improve Your Credit Book
Everything® Investing Book, 2nd Ed.
Everything® Landlording Book
Everything® Leadership Book
Everything® Managing People Book, 2nd Ed.
Everything® Negotiating Book
Everything® Online Auctions Book
Everything® Online Business Book
Everything® Personal Finance Book
Everything® Personal Finance in Your 20s and 30s Book
Everything® Project Management Book
Everything® Real Estate Investing Book
Everything® Retirement Planning Book
Everything® Robert's Rules Book, $7.95
Everything® Selling Book
Everything® Start Your Own Business Book, 2nd Ed.
Everything® Wills & Estate Planning Book

COOKING

Everything® Barbecue Cookbook
Everything® Bartender's Book, 2nd Ed., $9.95
Everything® Calorie Counting Cookbook
Everything® Cheese Book
Everything® Chinese Cookbook
Everything® Classic Recipes Book
Everything® Cocktail Parties & Drinks Book
Everything® College Cookbook
Everything® Cooking for Baby and Toddler Book
Everything® Cooking for Two Cookbook
Everything® Diabetes Cookbook
Everything® Easy Gourmet Cookbook
Everything® Fondue Cookbook
Everything® Fondue Party Book
Everything® Gluten-Free Cookbook
Everything® Glycemic Index Cookbook
Everything® Grilling Cookbook
Everything® Healthy Meals in Minutes Cookbook
Everything® Holiday Cookbook

Everything® Indian Cookbook
Everything® Italian Cookbook
Everything® Low-Carb Cookbook
Everything® Low-Cholesterol Cookbook
Everything® Low-Fat High-Flavor Cookbook
Everything® Low-Salt Cookbook
Everything® Meals for a Month Cookbook
Everything® Mediterranean Cookbook
Everything® Mexican Cookbook
Everything® No Trans Fat Cookbook
Everything® One-Pot Cookbook
Everything® Pizza Cookbook
Everything® Quick and Easy 30-Minute,
    5-Ingredient Cookbook
Everything® Quick Meals Cookbook
Everything® Slow Cooker Cookbook
Everything® Slow Cooking for a Crowd Cookbook
Everything® Soup Cookbook
Everything® Stir-Fry Cookbook
Everything® Sugar-Free Cookbook
Everything® Tapas and Small Plates Cookbook
Everything® Tex-Mex Cookbook
Everything® Thai Cookbook
Everything® Vegetarian Cookbook
Everything® Wild Game Cookbook
Everything® Wine Book, 2nd Ed.

GAMES

Everything® 15-Minute Sudoku Book, $9.95
Everything® 30-Minute Sudoku Book, $9.95
Everything® Bible Crosswords Book, $9.95
Everything® Blackjack Strategy Book
Everything® Brain Strain Book, $9.95
Everything® Bridge Book
Everything® Card Games Book
Everything® Card Tricks Book, $9.95
Everything® Casino Gambling Book, 2nd Ed.
Everything® Chess Basics Book
Everything® Craps Strategy Book
Everything® Crossword and Puzzle Book
Everything® Crossword Challenge Book
Everything® Crosswords for the Beach Book, $9.95
Everything® Cryptic Crosswords Book, $9.95
Everything® Cryptograms Book, $9.95
Everything® Easy Crosswords Book
Everything® Easy Kakuro Book, $9.95
Everything® Easy Large-Print Crosswords Book
Everything® Games Book, 2nd Ed.
Everything® Giant Sudoku Book, $9.95
Everything® Kakuro Challenge Book, $9.95
Everything® Large-Print Crossword Challenge Book
Everything® Large-Print Crosswords Book
Everything® Lateral Thinking Puzzles Book, $9.95

Everything® Literary Crosswords Book, $9.95
Everything® Mazes Book
Everything® Memory Booster Puzzles Book, $9.95
Everything® Movie Crosswords Book, $9.95
Everything® Music Crosswords Book, $9.95
Everything® Online Poker Book, $12.95
Everything® Pencil Puzzles Book, $9.95
Everything® Poker Strategy Book
Everything® Pool & Billiards Book
Everything® Puzzles for Commuters Book, $9.95
Everything® Sports Crosswords Book, $9.95
Everything® Test Your IQ Book, $9.95
Everything® Texas Hold 'Em Book, $9.95
Everything® Travel Crosswords Book, $9.95
Everything® TV Crosswords Book, $9.95
Everything® Word Games Challenge Book
Everything® Word Scramble Book
Everything® Word Search Book

HEALTH

Everything® Alzheimer's Book
Everything® Diabetes Book
Everything® Health Guide to Adult Bipolar Disorder
Everything® Health Guide to Arthritis
Everything® Health Guide to Controlling Anxiety
Everything® Health Guide to Fibromyalgia
Everything® Health Guide to Menopause
Everything® Health Guide to OCD
Everything® Health Guide to PMS
Everything® Health Guide to Postpartum Care
Everything® Health Guide to Thyroid Disease
Everything® Hypnosis Book
Everything® Low Cholesterol Book
Everything® Nutrition Book
Everything® Reflexology Book
Everything® Stress Management Book

HISTORY

Everything® American Government Book
Everything® American History Book, 2nd Ed.
Everything® Civil War Book
Everything® Freemasons Book
Everything® Irish History & Heritage Book
Everything® Middle East Book
Everything® World War II Book, 2nd Ed.

HOBBIES

Everything® Candlemaking Book
Everything® Cartooning Book
Everything® Coin Collecting Book
Everything® Drawing Book

Everything® Family Tree Book, 2nd Ed.
Everything® Knitting Book
Everything® Knots Book
Everything® Photography Book
Everything® Quilting Book
Everything® Sewing Book
Everything® Soapmaking Book, 2nd Ed.
Everything® Woodworking Book

HOME IMPROVEMENT

Everything® Feng Shui Book
Everything® Feng Shui Decluttering Book, $9.95
Everything® Fix-It Book
Everything® Green Living Book
Everything® Home Decorating Book
Everything® Home Storage Solutions Book
Everything® Homebuilding Book
Everything® Organize Your Home Book, 2nd Ed.

KIDS' BOOKS

All titles are $7.95

Everything® Kids' Animal Puzzle & Activity Book
Everything® Kids' Baseball Book, 4th Ed.
Everything® Kids' Bible Trivia Book
Everything® Kids' Bugs Book
Everything® Kids' Cars and Trucks Puzzle and Activity Book
Everything® Kids' Christmas Puzzle & Activity Book
Everything® Kids' Cookbook
Everything® Kids' Crazy Puzzles Book
Everything® Kids' Dinosaurs Book
Everything® Kids' Environment Book
Everything® Kids' Fairies Puzzle and Activity Book
Everything® Kids' First Spanish Puzzle and Activity Book
Everything® Kids' Gross Cookbook
Everything® Kids' Gross Hidden Pictures Book
Everything® Kids' Gross Jokes Book
Everything® Kids' Gross Mazes Book
Everything® Kids' Gross Puzzle & Activity Book
Everything® Kids' Halloween Puzzle & Activity Book
Everything® Kids' Hidden Pictures Book
Everything® Kids' Horses Book
Everything® Kids' Joke Book
Everything® Kids' Knock Knock Book
Everything® Kids' Learning Spanish Book
Everything® Kids' Magical Science Experiments Book
Everything® Kids' Math Puzzles Book
Everything® Kids' Mazes Book
Everything® Kids' Money Book
Everything® Kids' Nature Book
Everything® Kids' Pirates Puzzle and Activity Book
Everything® Kids' Presidents Book
Everything® Kids' Princess Puzzle and Activity Book
Everything® Kids' Puzzle Book
Everything® Kids' Racecars Puzzle and Activity Book
Everything® Kids' Riddles & Brain Teasers Book
Everything® Kids' Science Experiments Book
Everything® Kids' Sharks Book

Everything® Kids' Soccer Book
Everything® Kids' Spies Puzzle and Activity Book
Everything® Kids' States Book
Everything® Kids' Travel Activity Book

KIDS' STORY BOOKS

Everything® Fairy Tales Book

LANGUAGE

Everything® Conversational Japanese Book with CD, $19.95
Everything® French Grammar Book
Everything® French Phrase Book, $9.95
Everything® French Verb Book, $9.95
Everything® German Practice Book with CD, $19.95
Everything® Inglés Book
Everything® Intermediate Spanish Book with CD, $19.95
Everything® Italian Practice Book with CD, $19.95
Everything® Learning Brazilian Portuguese Book with CD, $19.95
Everything® Learning French Book with CD, 2nd Ed., $19.95
Everything® Learning German Book
Everything® Learning Italian Book
Everything® Learning Latin Book
Everything® Learning Russian Book with CD, $19.95
Everything® Learning Spanish Book with CD, 2nd Ed., $19.95
Everything® Russian Practice Book with CD, $19.95
Everything® Sign Language Book
Everything® Spanish Grammar Book
Everything® Spanish Phrase Book, $9.95
Everything® Spanish Practice Book with CD, $19.95
Everything® Spanish Verb Book, $9.95
Everything® Speaking Mandarin Chinese Book with CD, $19.95

MUSIC

Everything® Drums Book with CD, $19.95
Everything® Guitar Book with CD, 2nd Ed., $19.95
Everything® Guitar Chords Book with CD, $19.95
Everything® Home Recording Book
Everything® Music Theory Book with CD, $19.95
Everything® Reading Music Book with CD, $19.95
Everything® Rock & Blues Guitar Book with CD, $19.95
Everything® Rock and Blues Piano Book with CD, $19.95
Everything® Songwriting Book

NEW AGE

Everything® Astrology Book, 2nd Ed.
Everything® Birthday Personology Book
Everything® Dreams Book, 2nd Ed.
Everything® Love Signs Book, $9.95
Everything® Love Spells Book, $9.95
Everything® Numerology Book
Everything® Paganism Book
Everything® Palmistry Book
Everything® Psychic Book
Everything® Reiki Book
Everything® Sex Signs Book, $9.95

Everything® Spells & Charms Book, 2nd Ed.
Everything® Tarot Book, 2nd Ed.
Everything® Toltec Wisdom Book
Everything® Wicca and Witchcraft Book

PARENTING

Everything® Baby Names Book, 2nd Ed.
Everything® Baby Shower Book, 2nd Ed.
Everything® Baby's First Year Book
Everything® Birthing Book
Everything® Breastfeeding Book
Everything® Father-to-Be Book
Everything® Father's First Year Book
Everything® Get Ready for Baby Book, 2nd Ed.
Everything® Get Your Baby to Sleep Book, $9.95
Everything® Getting Pregnant Book
Everything® Guide to Pregnancy Over 35
Everything® Guide to Raising a One-Year-Old
Everything® Guide to Raising a Two-Year-Old
Everything® Guide to Raising Adolescent Boys
Everything® Guide to Raising Adolescent Girls
Everything® Homeschooling Book
Everything® Mother's First Year Book
Everything® Parent's Guide to Childhood Illnesses
Everything® Parent's Guide to Children and Divorce
Everything® Parent's Guide to Children with ADD/ADHD
Everything® Parent's Guide to Children with Asperger's Syndrome
Everything® Parent's Guide to Children with Autism
Everything® Parent's Guide to Children with Bipolar Disorder
Everything® Parent's Guide to Children with Depression
Everything® Parent's Guide to Children with Dyslexia
Everything® Parent's Guide to Children with Juvenile Diabetes
Everything® Parent's Guide to Positive Discipline
Everything® Parent's Guide to Raising a Successful Child
Everything® Parent's Guide to Raising Boys
Everything® Parent's Guide to Raising Girls
Everything® Parent's Guide to Raising Siblings
Everything® Parent's Guide to Sensory Integration Disorder
Everything® Parent's Guide to Tantrums
Everything® Parent's Guide to the Strong-Willed Child
Everything® Parenting a Teenager Book
Everything® Potty Training Book, $9.95
Everything® Pregnancy Book, 3rd Ed.
Everything® Pregnancy Fitness Book
Everything® Pregnancy Nutrition Book
Everything® Pregnancy Organizer, 2nd Ed., $16.95
Everything® Toddler Activities Book
Everything® Toddler Book
Everything® Tween Book
Everything® Twins, Triplets, and More Book

PETS

Everything® Aquarium Book
Everything® Boxer Book
Everything® Cat Book, 2nd Ed.
Everything® Chihuahua Book

Everything® **Cooking for Dogs Book**
Everything® Dachshund Book
Everything® Dog Book
Everything® Dog Health Book
Everything® Dog Obedience Book
Everything® Dog Owner's Organizer, $16.95
Everything® Dog Training and Tricks Book
Everything® German Shepherd Book
Everything® Golden Retriever Book
Everything® Horse Book
Everything® Horse Care Book
Everything® Horseback Riding Book
Everything® Labrador Retriever Book
Everything® Poodle Book
Everything® Pug Book
Everything® Puppy Book
Everything® Rottweiler Book
Everything® Small Dogs Book
Everything® Tropical Fish Book
Everything® Yorkshire Terrier Book

REFERENCE

Everything® American Presidents Book
Everything® Blogging Book
Everything® Build Your Vocabulary Book
Everything® Car Care Book
Everything® Classical Mythology Book
Everything® Da Vinci Book
Everything® Divorce Book
Everything® Einstein Book
Everything® Enneagram Book
Everything® Etiquette Book, 2nd Ed.
Everything® **Guide to Edgar Allan Poe**
Everything® Inventions and Patents Book
Everything® Mafia Book
Everything® **Martin Luther King Jr. Book**
Everything® Philosophy Book
Everything® Pirates Book
Everything® Psychology Book

RELIGION

Everything® Angels Book
Everything® Bible Book
Everything® **Bible Study Book with CD, $19.95**
Everything® Buddhism Book
Everything® Catholicism Book
Everything® Christianity Book
Everything® Gnostic Gospels Book
Everything® History of the Bible Book
Everything® Jesus Book
Everything® Jewish History & Heritage Book
Everything® Judaism Book
Everything® Kabbalah Book
Everything® Koran Book

Everything® Mary Book
Everything® Mary Magdalene Book
Everything® Prayer Book
Everything® Saints Book, 2nd Ed.
Everything® Torah Book
Everything® Understanding Islam Book
Everything® **Women of the Bible Book**
Everything® World's Religions Book
Everything® Zen Book

SCHOOL & CAREERS

Everything® Alternative Careers Book
Everything® Career Tests Book
Everything® College Major Test Book
Everything® College Survival Book, 2nd Ed.
Everything® Cover Letter Book, 2nd Ed.
Everything® Filmmaking Book
Everything® Get-a-Job Book, 2nd Ed.
Everything® Guide to Being a Paralegal
Everything® Guide to Being a Personal Trainer
Everything® Guide to Being a Real Estate Agent
Everything® Guide to Being a Sales Rep
Everything® **Guide to Being an Event Planner**
Everything® Guide to Careers in Health Care
Everything® Guide to Careers in Law Enforcement
Everything® Guide to Government Jobs
Everything® **Guide to Starting and Running a Catering Business**
Everything® Guide to Starting and Running a Restaurant
Everything® Job Interview Book
Everything® New Nurse Book
Everything® New Teacher Book
Everything® Paying for College Book
Everything® Practice Interview Book
Everything® Resume Book, 2nd Ed.
Everything® Study Book

SELF-HELP

Everything® **Body Language Book**
Everything® Dating Book, 2nd Ed.
Everything® Great Sex Book
Everything® Self-Esteem Book
Everything® Tantric Sex Book

SPORTS & FITNESS

Everything® Easy Fitness Book
Everything® **Krav Maga for Fitness Book**
Everything® Running Book

TRAVEL

Everything® **Family Guide to Coastal Florida**
Everything® Family Guide to Cruise Vacations
Everything® Family Guide to Hawaii
Everything® Family Guide to Las Vegas, 2nd Ed.
Everything® Family Guide to Mexico
Everything® Family Guide to New York City, 2nd Ed.
Everything® Family Guide to RV Travel & Campgrounds
Everything® Family Guide to the Caribbean
Everything® **Family Guide to the Disneyland® Resort, California Adventure®, Universal Studios®, and the Anaheim Area, 2nd Ed.**
Everything® **Family Guide to the Walt Disney World Resort®, Universal Studios®, and Greater Orlando, 5th Ed.**
Everything® Family Guide to Timeshares
Everything® Family Guide to Washington D.C., 2nd Ed.

WEDDINGS

Everything® Bachelorette Party Book, $9.95
Everything® Bridesmaid Book, $9.95
Everything® Destination Wedding Book
Everything® Elopement Book, $9.95
Everything® Father of the Bride Book, $9.95
Everything® Groom Book, $9.95
Everything® Mother of the Bride Book, $9.95
Everything® Outdoor Wedding Book
Everything® Wedding Book, 3rd Ed.
Everything® Wedding Checklist, $9.95
Everything® Wedding Etiquette Book, $9.95
Everything® Wedding Organizer, 2nd Ed., $16.95
Everything® Wedding Shower Book, $9.95
Everything® Wedding Vows Book, $9.95
Everything® Wedding Workout Book
Everything® **Weddings on a Budget Book, 2nd Ed., $9.95**

WRITING

Everything® Creative Writing Book
Everything® Get Published Book, 2nd Ed.
Everything® Grammar and Style Book
Everything® Guide to Magazine Writing
Everything® Guide to Writing a Book Proposal
Everything® Guide to Writing a Novel
Everything® Guide to Writing Children's Books
Everything® Guide to Writing Copy
Everything® **Guide to Writing Graphic Novels**
Everything® Guide to Writing Research Papers
Everything® Screenwriting Book
Everything® Writing Poetry Book
Everything® Writing Well Book